The British Churches Turn to the Future

also published by SCM Press

The British Churches Today
by Kenneth Slack

The Future of the Christian Church
by Arthur Michael Ramsey and Leon-Joseph Suenens

Christians in a New World
edited by David L. Edwards

Christians and the Common Market
a report presented to the British Council of Churches

The Search for Security: A Christian Appraisal
a report to the British Council of Churches

DAVID L. EDWARDS

The British Churches Turn to the Future

One Man's View of the Church Leaders' Conference Birmingham 1972

SCM PRESS LTD

To the memory of

IAN RAMSEY

philosopher and bishop

whose life disclosed to many

what the truth is in Jesus

334 00141 2

First published 1973
by SCM Press Ltd
56 Bloomsbury Street London
Second impression 1973

Printed in Great Britain by
Fletcher & Son Ltd, Norwich

CONTENTS

PREFACE

This is an account and assessment of an unprecedented event: the Church Leaders' Conference organized by the British Council of Churches with a substantial Roman Catholic participation in the Selly Oak Colleges, Birmingham, from 11 to 20 September 1972.

It is a personal document, claiming no authority. From the start the conference was intended to be an honest meeting of 500 minds – not an assembly, synod or council attempting to legislate, polishing up resolutions or issuing a carefully agreed message. As it turned out, it was even more informal than had been planned, for the conference decided to spend more time in the eight commissions into which it was divided and less time in plenary sessions for corporate debate. It is in accordance with the spirit of the conference that I should give a general impression rather than all the details, and state my own reactions frankly.

On the other hand, the publication of a report to the British and Irish Churches and to anyone else interested was part of the plan agreed to by the British Council of Churches and by the representatives of the Roman Catholic Church, and publication of this book had been announced, according to plan, before the conference met. Every facility and freedom have been given to me by the officers, staff and members of the conference, and I am deeply grateful for the honour. Although I am alone responsible for the contents of this report, it could not have been written without such co-operation.

I

Learning through Meeting

'Not Just Talk'

At the conference I am going to describe, many people caught a vision of the future of Christianity in Britain and Ireland. For example, the English Free Church leader, Dr Kenneth Greet, Secretary of the Methodist Conference, declared: 'Most, surely, will recognize the will of God in a new pattern of leadership – a leadership which listens ... As the word "collegiality" edges its way into our vocabulary, the hand on the helm will become steadier. And maybe the conditions for a new Pentecost will be created ... I came here believing church union to be right; I go away believing it to be inevitable ... I believe God has revealed to us more clearly our resources in faith ... The reward of accepting the disciplines of ecumenical encounter is a richer understanding ... My judgment is that God will send no one away empty from this conference.'

Such an assessment may seem extravagant. It was made at the last session of the Church Leaders' Conference, and there was a holiday feeling in the air after nine days of intensive and complex discussions. But its worst critic could never accuse this conference of being complacent. The Archbishop of Canterbury, Dr Michael Ramsey, was heard saying that it was the only large conference he had ever really enjoyed, but his own public assessment of the proceedings showed that if there was joy to be had at 'Birmingham 1972' it was the joy of an honest struggle with problems.

Deep divisions were emphasized. Conservatives and radicals seemed to have utterly different conceptions of the church. The theological split revealed was almost one between two Christianities. But this open controversy between Christians was not the main battle. The real fight was seen to be against secularism, and often the Christian church seemed to be losing it. The impact of secularization in thought and life was often felt as overwhelming, while the church's own attitudes were often shown to be confused. Confident adherents of particular theologies or schools of churchmanship, Catholic or Evangelical, orthodox or modernist, had their say – only to impress others with their inadequacy. The listening which the assembled leaders did was often painful, and any richer understanding was reached only through the discipline of an encounter that was not far from a little death. Kenneth Greet said: 'It would be very strange, indeed quite terrible, if for all of us in this conference there had not been moments when we had nothing to offer to God but a broken spirit and a contrite heart.'

The Archbishop of Canterbury addressed the conference with some of the strangest encouragement ever offered to a gathering of British and Irish church leaders. 'I want to say how very grateful indeed I am for having been here ... This has been a conference that has known and acknowledged deep frustration and despair and yet has found glimmers of faith in the midst of that frustration and despair.'

'I believe that this is an experience very near to the heart of Christian faith itself,' the Archbishop continued. 'Christian faith is that something happens in the midst of despair and shows up – just as shadows of despair keep falling across faith ... I am grateful for a conference which has had unusual openness and vigour in the meeting and sharing of minds and spirits about the meaning of Christian faith in theological terms and about the corollaries of Christian faith for the urgent action of Christians ... While we have as usual been talking, we have had an unusual degree of scepticism about talk ... because we have been in an atmosphere of worship and the sense of obligations and obedience. I believe that under God it is the presence of that sense that has given to some of the talking the quality of not being just talk.'

The Reasons for the Conference

The conference was unprecedented, for the crisis it faced is without precedent. The recent statistics of decline in church attendance, membership and finance are alarming to anyone who is in any way involved in the organization of the Christian religion in Britain and Ireland, but most thoughtful observers expect worse statistics to come, the question being whether frustration and despair will grow.

The average age in the congregations and the clergy is high, and the contempt of most young people for the institutional life of the church is the harder for churchmen to bear because the younger generation often seems interested both in the ecstasies of the mystical consciousness and in the practical obligations of the struggle for a just and humane society. The alienation of this new generation will, if unchecked, bring greater and greater disasters as the church's ageing leadership and membership die, and as those who are now young discover alternative ways of being religious.

Ireland, where secularization has so far been milder than anywhere else in these islands, will be the scene of a more militant rebellion against the rival churches as more and more young people realize how much poison has been injected into the national life by prejudices which have very often been encouraged by religious sentiments. In Ireland during the 1970s 'Catholic' and 'Protestant' have been words accompanying hatred, riots, burnings and murders, and the daily tragedies reported throughout Britain and the world have sickened millions with this disgusting legacy of religion. And even where the decline of the churches in the public's respect is less bloodstained and therefore less anguished, it still seems bound to be widely devastating. This is not only true of the English Free Churches, although they are the worst hit. The Roman Catholic Church, which so far has more or less held its own statistically, has entered an internal crisis of authority, brought to a head by the laity's virtual rejection of the heirarchy's teaching on birth control – and by the defection of a sizeable number of able priests for conscience sake. This confusion seems likely to grow unless a new model of spiritual authority can be understood and accepted. Even the Church of Scotland, which has prospered as the national church, shows symptoms which alarm her more thoughtful sons, while the nationalist resurgence in Wales has not led to a return to the churches and chapels.

Finance would be enough by itself to cause alarm, even in the Church of England, where endowments are massive but inadequate for maintenance, let alone advance. The present rate of inflation means that prices will double every fifteen years or so. The incomes of the churches and of their supporters are not doubling. Everywhere the churches are having to economize. In a way, it is fortunate that fewer candidates for ordination come forward. If more young men offered themselves, the churches could not afford to accept them.

But the alarming statistics show only parts of the crisis, for the basic problem confronting the churches in the 1970s is unbelief. Doctrines held for many centuries – and still held by many – to be fundamental to Christian faith increasingly appear incredible. The doctrine of chastity outside marriage seems remote to a generation well stimulated by commercial erotica, well cautioned against sexual repression, and well equipped with contraceptives. The doctrines of turning the other cheek and loving the enemy seem more appropriate to fairyland than to the world which is real to this generation because it appears every night on television – a world which preserves its peace through the incessant blackmail of nuclear weapons, which achieves some affluence because it fails to provide enough food for two-thirds, which carries on the Olympic Games after the murder of the Israeli athletes; and which is helpless before a racism as brutal in Uganda as in South Africa. Many of the doctrines about Christ himself seem incomprehensible except as echoes from childhood's Christmas. Even the doctrine of the heavenly Father, so easily parodied by the picture of the grandfather in the sky, is to many a fantasy in a universe of terrifying scale and randomness. More and more people in our day appear to be rejecting all these doctrines, some with a wistful nostalgia but others with impatience or unconcern.

Meanwhile the Christian church's once proud doctrines about its own life seem to belong to libraries or to those sheltered and obscure places where the life otherwise entombed in libraries can be brought out for a ritual dance. Attempts at the revision or restatement of the old doctrines suffer from great confusion, for in the church the most loyal members seem to be the most suspicious of theology, while the most intelligent seem the most worried. Theologians retreat into impenetrable jargon or throw themselves suicidally into secular fashions. The Church Leaders' Conference met a few months after the publication of a Penguin paperback, *The Way of Transcendence*, in which Dr Alastair Kee, Lecturer in Theology in the University of Hull, argued that in order to survive Christianity must openly abandon belief in God. The conference had the theme 'Discovering God's Will Together', but it was not long before the sly remark went round: the theologians have heard about the death of God, and now they are looking for his will.

The contrast between the alarmed conservatism of much church life and the pace of modernity in the world is startling. The thinking of churchmen about society has been largely outmoded by the breathless history of the last few years. Suddenly millions have awakened to the threat of pollution and exhaustion of natural resources – but no major church conference in Britain before this had studied the subject. Britain is busy creating new towns and a new pattern of life in the old ones – but the churches, having contributed few initiatives to the planning, have found it difficult to stretch themselves so as to cover the new reality. The elaborate machinery of the churches, designed for the conduct of ordered worship and the pastoral care of a settled neighbourhood, has not been moved fast enough to meet this swift social change. Church budgets can provide little more than token support of experiments to reach out to where the modern layman lives, or to sustain an informed commentary on new social problems and ethical issues. No clear and strong Christian critique of our present economic system has yet emerged – although there is general agreement that in rich countries such as Britain workers continue to feel that the only reality about their work is the money grudgingly paid for the use of their hands by the hour, and although the contrast between the affluent white sector and the coloured majority of mankind grows wider and more embittered, with the world's population doubling every thirty years. The revolutionary rate of change in our times, with all its promises and threats, usually seems to pass the churches by.

It may be of interest to recall that it was my experience of the gulf fixed between the church and the modern world that led me to suggest the idea of the Church Leaders' Conference. For a time I was Dean of King's College, Cambridge. King's College Chapel, as large as some cathedrals, is more beautiful (I think) than any. Beside the river and the Cambridge Backs, it stands as it was completed in almost flawless perfection immediately before the English Reformation. But it is, after all, a college chapel. While I served the college as its Dean or senior chaplain, the Provost of King's, Dr Edmund Leach, broadcast some Reith Lectures on *A Runaway World*, gladly accepting the idea of the death of God. The contrast between the traditional beauty of King's College Chapel and the runaway secularism of King's College naturally occupied my mind. It was thought-provoking to move from Evensong immaculately performed by the world-famous choir in the candlelight, via dinner with humorously sceptical colleagues, to the students' blaring and sweating discotheque in a concrete cellar, but this contrast seemed only to symbolize the whole precarious position of the church, left amid secular change like the skeleton of a dinosaur. And when I was elected to the Administrative Committee of the British Council of Churches, I determined to use this position to persuade the leaders of the churches to think harder about the basic problems.

I wanted them to apply their minds more strenuously to the crisis of faith and to the crisis of the institutional church, because I guessed that their minds were in fact preoccupied with short-term administrative and pastoral problems. It must be tempting for a church leader to concentrate on the maintenance of a network of churches and on the worries of those who run or attend those churches, leaving the world to its own devices. These busy men – and the few women who fall into this category – say that they do not read much, and although almost all of them are dedicated pastors, the conversations which they have with laymen seldom seem to be of a tone which expresses the world's sharpest questions to the church. The laymen they meet are too respectful. I respected these bishops and suchlike; when I met them, they seemed to be in a better moral and spiritual condition than I was. But since, like some others, I looked to them for leadership, I wanted to see them grappling with contemporary reality.

I had attended and admired the first British Conference on 'Faith and Order', organized by the British Council of Churches in Nottingham in 1964; indeed, with a Methodist collaborator, Rupert Davies, I had written the report on that meeting, *Unity Begins at Home*. But that conference had been deliberately ecclesiastical, within the assumptions of the traditionally Christian thought-world. It had also consisted largely of those enthusiasts called ecumeniacs. I now wanted a conference about truth rather than unity; and a conference of people selected not by any ecumenical body but by their own churches because they were people with responsibility and influence.

When I put up the idea of a Church Leaders' Conference, in a memorandum written on the last day of 1969, I found no opposition at all. Only two criticisms came. The first was that I was thinking too much in English terms. Originally I wanted a kind of English Council of Churches to sponsor an event where the dominant figure would be the Archbishop of Canterbury. However, the British Council of Churches is the only official inter-church body that exists apart from local councils in England, and in the discussions at the BCC it soon became clear that Scotland, Wales and Ireland must be included, simply because their representatives were interested. Moreover, the Archbishop of Canterbury, while throwing the weight of his blessing behind the project, insisted that he would prefer to listen rather than to lecture. Another criticism which I accepted was that my original scheme was too intellectual. The BCC has concentrated on the relationship between Christian faith and the political and social questions of the day. A solid achievement of relevant comment has been built up (as is now shown by Dr Ernest Payne's short history of *Thirty Years of the British Council of Churches*). Both members and staff of the Council rightly insisted that the proposed conference should be opened to a wide range of social concerns.

So my proposal was enriched. A further widening of the debate came quickly when the Joint Working Group of the Council of Churches and the Roman Catholic Church, formed in 1967 by the BCC and the hierarchies of England and Wales, and of Scotland, said that a similar idea had been forming in its mind, to enable Roman Catholic leaders to meet others on an equal footing. In the event, the Church Leaders' Conference included forty officially appointed Roman Catholic members, and it met only a few months after the publication of a careful document setting out the implications of possible Roman Catholic membership of the British Council of Churches. Already Roman Catholic churches belong to about three-quarters of the local councils affiliated to the BCC, and whenever Roman Catholic leaders express an interest in joint discussions or activities at the national level, either as consultant-observers or as full members, the great majority of BCC members and supporters take it for granted that they will be welcomed. I have never succeeded in overcoming my astonishment that the Roman Catholic Church, which I (as an Anglican made a priest before John XXIII was made a pope) used to regard as rigid and monolithic, should be so kindly disposed towards other Christians, and so much at the heart of the ecumenical movement for renewal and reunion; but whenever I have met this phenomenon, I have never been able to do anything else than give thanks for the most hopeful part of the Christian scene in this age.

One conclusion which I drew from my experience, even before I went to Birmingham for the conference, was that the leaders of the British churches are in a humble mood. They are, indeed, far more self-critical than our secular leaders. Carried to an extreme, this can be one more weakness in the church (as an MP who was present pointed out to the conference). But it can also be a ground of hope. As someone else remarked at the conference, books are no longer written with titles such as *The Claims of the Church of ...* A more fashionable title would be *The Concerns of ...* More fashionable – and more Christian.

Another lesson which I learned was that when an individual, however insignificant, believes in the churches sufficiently to ask them politely to do something which they can do, that man can be humiliated – not by indifference but by the churches' humility in seeking to discover the will of God amid their own failures and sins.

And a third lesson I learned was that if they have the will the churches can do a lot with a little, because they can still draw on a great fund of co-operation and self-sacrifice. In the political or commercial world, any exercise so novel and ambitious as the Church Leaders' Conference would have involved heavy expenditure. In this case, however, all the costs had to be recovered from the fee of £30 charged for each delegate (and from a collection taken to pay for the concerts, films and theatre evening), and the conference had to be planned without the help of a single full-time employee. In the end, because backers were generous a little profit was made – and because volunteers were generous the BCC staff was not overburdened.

The chairman of the conference, John Huxtable, was the chief official (Minister-Secretary) of the Congregational Church in England and Wales, and was in the throes of the last preparations for the union of that Church with the Presbyterian Church of England to form the United Reformed Church. (The actual union took place in Westminster on 5 October.) The chairman of the team which directed the study of the conference, and of its steering committee, was Dr Kenneth Slack, a man prominently involved in the same unity scheme and with another heavy load of work, as the Minister of the City Temple in London. The secretary of the conference, responsible for all its administrative detail, was Michael Hubbard, a third Congregationalist – and himself a busy pastor, as the Minister of Carr's Lane Church, the newly rebuilt equivalent of the City Temple in Birmingham. He was assisted by Verleigh Cant, who also gave much time to the secretarial work of the World Council of Churches' Central Committee. Such people worked for the conference because they were convinced of its necessity.

No less essential to the conference was the personal welcome and service given to it by many members of the Staff of the Selly Oak Colleges, led by their President, Paul Rowntree Clifford. This cluster of colleges in a suburb of Birmingham near the Bournville works proved to be not only an almost ideal location, enabling the delegates to build up a family spirit in the various colleges where they stayed. It was also a model, showing what could be done when Christians co-operated with each other and with 'secular' bodies for the sake of a mission and service reaching out into all the world. The Selly Oak 'federation' was formed in 1922 by six colleges which had been founded during and since 1903 (on a rock made of Cadbury's chocolate, it might be said – inaccurately in most cases), mainly for missionary and teacher training and other forms of Christian adult education. Since then the Church of England's two main missionary societies have both moved their training centres to Selly Oak, and the training of social workers has grown, including courses sponsored by the British government for overseas social workers. Most of the training of missionaries is now done on an ecumenical basis, with a distinguished central staff, but Selly Oak also has pupils under its own Reader in Islamics, and is building both a centre to train teachers for the mentally handicapped and 'Prospect Hall' for the education of physically handicapped adults. Every term it houses about 800 students, drawn from many cultures and faiths and from over fifty countries. Some of the talents assembled were displayed in two concerts arranged by the Director of Music, William Bulman.

No place in Britain or Ireland could have offered more hospitality or inspiration to this Church Leaders' Conference.

A Sticky Start

The conference met for the first time in the George Cadbury Hall on Monday 11 September 1972. But its start was sticky, and it is interesting to see why. There was an explosion of discontent on the Thursday, at a session which had been planned to be the first of two sessions discussing 'The Real Issues before the Church: Is the Conference Facing Them?' As a result of this candid criticism, the programme was radically revised. Further sessions intended to be led by panels on the platform were abandoned, and it was arranged that the commissions into which the conference was divided should report to each other, only briefly presenting their work to a plenary session. It was later agreed that the conference should pass no resolutions at all. Instead of giving time to corporate deliberations, the conference welcomed its Steering Committee's new plans for one session when contrasting theologians would meet in dialogue and be questioned, and two sessions for members to speak from their hearts about the cause of Christian unity.

The officers of the conference, with others appointed by the BCC, had consulted on several occasions personally (and more by letter) with the equally busy people invited to lecture, to give Bible studies or to lead the commissions. But inevitably the programme drawn up in these London meetings was open to criticism, and with an equal inevitability it received it when 500 people got together in Birmingham, most of them being used to arranging their own conferences or other meetings. Had the planning committees in London proposed an entirely flexible conference, with few lectures or other plenary sessions and the general motto 'Leave it to the Spirit', the members of the conference might well have objected that their time was being wasted on chat with no clear agenda – if they had been ready to sacrifice the time to a project so nebulous. Or, had they turned up, these church leaders might have discussed banalities and trivialities, lacking the stimulus to probe deeper. In fact the committees, after some consideration of alternatives, decided that in the printed brochure quite a heavy programme of thought and work should be outlined, and only a few sessions left blank. The discontent that welled up in the George Cadbury Hall therefore accused the organizers of having organized too much.

With the advantage of hindsight, those who had planned the programme acknowledged that they had assumed too readily that the pattern of plenary debates which had been memorably successful at the Nottingham Conference in 1964 could be repeated eight years later. They had been too amiable in considering the draft programme put forward by one committee member (myself) who – incredible as this may seem – was engaged at that time in writing a book which praised some of the Victorian leaders of religious life and thought. Possibly half-hoping that the conference might witness the resurrection of a few Victorian giants, the planners had not paid enough attention to the growing preference for small, informal groups. They had not taken seriously enough the 'group dynamics' imported from America, or the lively methods now used to make adult education palatable.

This failure belonged to a wider failure in the churches to evolve a new style of leadership and initiative. The subject of 'leadership' had not been put on the formal agenda of this Church Leaders' Conference, but it quickly came to the fore. The revolt against the printed programme sprang in part from a frustration in the churches over the practical working out of 'collegiality', 'synodical government' and the 'church meeting'. The Victorian style of leadership is now outmoded, but has not been replaced. All too often the actual meetings produced by these fine new principles are boring, because in them the creative, corporate spirit is not noticeable. 'We cannot lead,' said David Jenkins in an illuminating aside during his lecture; 'the question is how we can be set free to follow.' Michael Hare-Duke, Bishop of St Andrews in the Episcopal Church, had some reflections published during the conference in *The Scotsman*.

'This problem of authority is one which seems almost to bedevil our whole society,' he wrote. 'If such are the dilemmas of the political world or of industry as men seek to grasp authority, they are no less urgent problems for the churches. In the course of history the same patterns of authority have been exercised in the name of God as in the name of Mammon. Every institution which exists in time must have some sort of structure. There are bound to be appointed chairmen; if things are to be done, a group must form itself into some kind of a committee. But these are ways of achieving ends; never ends in themselves. The task of those who are given formal authority may very often be only that of keeping the procedural bonds sufficiently loose to allow the man who has the real word of God to break in and set a new course.

'Such a pattern depends upon the qualities of humility in all who hold office so that they may be willing to see others as the real makers of the future. It requires courage for those who have a vision to break through old structures which hinder and hold back new movement. In writing of this one is not only thinking of new possibilities for the Christian denominations but also of a model which might in fact deeply affect the workings of our society.'

Some blame, therefore, attached to the conference's planners. But some responsibility for the difficulties in its early days should be claimed by its members, who found themselves inadequately prepared for the shocks and strains. All members had been asked to read three books. Two of these described the current situations in church life and religious thought: *The British Churches Today* by Kenneth Slack and my own *Religion and Change*. The third was more visionary: *The Future of the Christian Church*, lectures by Michael Ramsey, Archbishop of Canterbury, and Cardinal Leon-Joseph Suenens, Archbishop of Malines – Brussels. However, the reading that had been done had evidently not been enough; perhaps the wrong books had been chosen. Nor had the material supplied or recommended to every commission proved an adequate supplement. In the face-to-face meetings in Birmingham, many members of the conference were to a greater or lesser extent distressed by prolonged exposure to arguments and traditions not their own. The criticism of this gathering as 'just another conference' was singularly inaccurate. It included some veterans of many ecumenical meetings, but for most of its members Birmingham 1972 was the first such experience, apart from brief, local get-togethers.

Many people were puzzled by the donnish style of the radical lecturers; Bishop Ramsey seemed to be 'disappearing into the clouds in the general direction of God', and Canon Jenkins seemed to do little except ask questions and crack jokes. The more radical members were dismayed by Cardinal Heenan's hard doctrine and by the 'torrents of Torrance' (the militantly orthodox Professor T. F. Torrance). It all took a good deal of sitting through. All the lecturers talked too much, given that audience. But the audience, too, had something to learn, about theology – and although most had the sense to listen, not all these church leaders resisted the temptation to complain about minor points or simply talk about something else. The radicals who were so critical of church leadership were guilty of a similar evasion; the seven mottoes which were produced from these younger quarters at the end of the conference, to sum it all up, did not contain a single reference to theology or a single statement which was specifically Christian. The audience, once released, enjoyed discussing the strong personalities which had appeared on the theological platform, but the difficulties felt in absorbing the intellectual food on offer suggested that the British may be incapable of digesting theology except through the straw of gossip.

There was also stress in the life of the conference outside the plenary sessions. Presumably if one is a Roman Catholic bishop, one is not accustomed to sit at table day after day with talkatively heretical Protestants. If one is an activist eager to bring down the South African government, one has to conquer one's impatience with a sweet but almost silent nun. If one is wondering all the time how the parish is getting on, one has to make an effort to enter an argument about Irish politics. Many members of the conference found that their baptism in the full ecumenical experience meant being immersed in chilly waters.

At times they could not help wishing that they were back in their own studies or offices, surrounded by books they could shut up or secretaries to whom they could dictate. Nor could they help thinking of the homes they could have been visiting as Fathers-in-God, instead of arguing about ideas in a conference. One passage in Cardinal Heenan's address was equally well received by conservatives and by radicals alike: his attack on conferences as distractions from practical duties. 'A parish priest,' he recalled out of his own long experience as one, 'must keep his eye on the ball.' One priest present at the time took the hint. Father Anthony Ross, OP, who had been chosen to lead the commission on social and pastoral work ('Caring for People in Crisis') because of his outstanding effectiveness as a pastor, left the conference in the midst of its crisis in order to resume his work in Edinburgh. (Before he abandoned his commission, he had the experience of being denounced by a nun for dereliction of duty.) Kenneth Greet made some shrewd observations about the dangers and hesitations. 'It was a dangerous thing to call this conference. If 500 church leaders gathered to discover God's will, and nothing happened, that could itself be most significant. It might mean that God was dead, or that the disciples were dead – so the critics would say. Moreover, contrary to popular notions, most of us who came did so unwillingly. It is a busy time of the year for people like us. I never heard so much moaning at the bar – and elsewhere – about the time involved.'

The conference was the most representative gathering of church leaders assembled in Britain or Ireland since the Reformation. But it was not allowed to pride itself on its inclusiveness. Each day a duplicated sheet of paper, usually yellow, was handed to members as they entered the George Cadbury Hall for Bible study to begin the conference day. Instead of listening to the recorded Mozart, or silently contemplating their Bibles, most members could be seen studying the yellow sheet before the lecturer began his biblical exposition. For this newsletter, entitled *Upside*, was prepared by younger and more radical members, who had been for the most part invited to the conference by the BCC as guaranteed trouble-makers and who were now collected together by the movement called 'One for Christian Renewal'. And one of the complaints of those who quite rightly wished to turn the world upside down was that the churches had not sent more people like them as representatives. Why were there so many grey heads? Why so few women? Why only seventy laymen? (Whether more laymen would have welcomed being sent to the conference is another question. One who was there remarked that after so much religion he deserved six months' leave from churchgoing.) Why so few agnostics? Why did the conference on its afternoon off hire buses to enjoy an outing to Coventry Cathedral, or to be entertained by the monks of Prinknash Abbey in that exquisite country overlooking Gloucester, instead of identifying with the poor in Birmingham? The abrasive paragraphs of *Upside* included attacks on the conference's Steering Committee, and named the guilty men; but even those church leaders who escaped personal attack were made liable to pangs of guilt for being what they were.

Not only youth criticized the churches for sending to Birmingham the men they did send. Kenneth Greet – whose graciousness in closing the conference contrasted with *Upside* – made a point of lamenting the churches' failure to send more women. 'We must, I think, take very seriously the unrepresentative nature of this gathering. Male dominance is one of the most pervasive and disastrous defects in the whole Christian tradition. The equal partnership of men and women is plainly the mark of that true humanity which is God's design and purpose. The practical denial of it has resulted in all manner of error and dire impoverishment.'

So both the planners and the members of the conference stood – or (worse) *sat* – convicted. But a part of the blame for the conference's sticky start should certainly be attached to the problems themselves. Intellectual and social challenges were jumbled together confusingly. Was sociology irrelevant to questions of religious truth, as Cardinal Heenan seemed to maintain, or did it help churchmen to see realities, as he was told? Was it the basic problem that Christianity often seemed to be untrue, or at least to be so badly stated as to be incredible? Or did it matter more that the Christian church was too closely identified with the rich and the white?

In boxing with such problems, no punches were pulled. For example, a panel on 'Spiritual Life Today' (presided over by the genial Cardinal Gray, Archbishop of St Andrews and Edinburgh) was presented from the floor with a straight-forward challenge about the value of the Christian tradition of intercessory prayer – and gave no clear answer except that 'intercessory' was the wrong word to use.

All of the four lecturers mentioned earlier spoke with uncommon frankness and seemed unconcerned to woo their opponents. This mood was inaugurated by the Head of the Civil Service, Sir William Armstrong, who surprised his audience and also his cautious subordinates back in Whitehall by the candour of his theme that nowadays he seldom went to church and seldom missed it. The gentlest lecturer, Bishop Janani Luwum, did not discuss the crisis in his own country, Uganda (for reasons which the conference understood well), but he did speak frankly of the Third World's disappointment at Britain's ('the Mother Country's') withdrawal into itself; while the most confident speaker, the Right Honourable Peter Walker, then Secretary of State for the Environment, did not conceal his belief that the face of Britain was being changed by forces other than the churches.

Already in the opening service of the conference, the preacher, Derrick Greeves, Minister of St Andrew's Methodist Church, Worcester, issued a warning. He spoke 'as something that has crawled out from under the grass-roots'. He spoke directly of the loneliness, frustrations and 'giant agony' of church leadership in this time. He voiced a sense of sin which pierced the heart.

'Far from having a *carte blanche*, you have a tangled skein of threads to unravel,' he said. 'Part of the strain on church leaders at the moment is due to the fact that so many are saying, "What a mess you're in!" The whole church is suffering from analysis paralysis. And like leaders in every sphere of life today, church leaders are being offered a spate of criticism and advice – as though they were football managers whose teams were failing to score goals. I for one would often be on the side of the critics, but it's no easy thing for a leader to decide what advice to heed and what to ignore. Tidy up your dogmas! Trim your structures! Change your vocabulary! Bury God! Sell your jewels and burn your buildings! Tear up your letters patent as priests! Admit that morals have collapsed like a cliff-edge!

'We're all besotted, punch-drunk, with words. Pamphlets and paperbacks are as thick as confetti in the church porch. Television spokesmen cry, "Where is your God?" Journalists question the church's authority even to hold an opinion. The church leader, like Moses, is "burdened with the care of this people", and just when the burden is heaviest, he's treated like a sick man who overhears people talking about him as though he were dead.

'Who can blame a leader for being worried about how he is prospering? How am I doing? But a leader is finished if his one obsession is about his own image. Sometimes nowadays the church is like a self-conscious bride, as though the Bride of Christ were trying to do herself up for the congregation. In fact the Bride of Christ will never look good enough. Her only beauty is in the eye of the Bridegroom. Church leaders are not called upon to satisfy the electorate, or to worry too much about what anyone but Jesus thinks of them. Jesus talks about the sign and token of leadership being that the world hates you. So this conference is an honest-to-goodness turning away from the individualist strains and tensions, and the lonely, private-study search for the truth, away from obsessions about what our image is in the eyes of the world – a turning away from all this to find what God is saying in the happenings of our time.

'Heaven forbid that out of this conference there should come a high-powered campaign to try to make the churches penitent. Before we knew where we were, we should all be walking into the SPCK bookshop, and asking, "Have you got a copy of *I'm Sorry, God* and *United Penitential Psalms* – and a sackcloth cassock – and a stone from Gethsemane to kneel on?" Some people talk as if "turning again and walking humbly with God" were a simple possibility. But it's just this that we cannot do to order. Repentance is a gift of God given in response to our sense of desperate need to begin again.

'Repentance in the Bible always means a change of course, sometimes, as Alan Richardson says, in a morally neutral sense. But it always means changing one's mind and going in another direction. Repentance means ringing up the doctor when at last you face the fact that you cannot cure yourself. It means actually setting out from the far country – the tears come later. It means deliberately climbing up a hill to discover God's will for that day.'

The Spirit Moves

What happened at the Church Leaders' Conference was that, after repentance of that kind, the Holy Spirit took control.

I am astonished to find myself writing such a sentence. Like many other Christians, I have been reluctant to say much about the Holy Spirit, because I have been too well aware of the follies committed in this name. As a student of church history I have to reject any claim, however official, that the church has been made infallible by the guidance of the Holy Spirit. As a student of the Bible I also know that the scriptures, however holy, are not infallible. But I have been no less embarrassed by the claims of Christians who are not great churchgoers or readers. The picture of an enthusiast 'speaking with tongues' does not excite me, for I think it more important that people should have a horror of talking nonsense, and that emotionalism should be subordinated to self-control and practical kindness. Being sceptical about many claims to possess the Spirit, I felt my mind strangely warmed when Dr Richard Hanson (then Bishop of Clogher in Ireland, but soon to be Professor of Theology in Manchester) devoted part of a Bible study to showing that the Acts of the Apostles gives no more than a picturesque account of the gift of the Spirit on that feast of Pentecost which was the first Whit Sunday.

But my heart moved when some local Jesus Kids sang to the delegates as they met for the first time, and distributed *Jesus is alive today* stickers for the church leaders to wear – and when the Roman Catholic Archbishop of Birmingham read the simple promise of the Spirit at the conference's opening service: 'Is there a father among you who will offer his son a snake when he asks for fish, or a scorpion when he asks for an egg? If you then, bad as you are, know how to give your children what is good for them, how much more will the heavenly father give the Holy Spirit to those who ask him!'

When an Anglican bishop told me that the conference had taught him that the Pentecostal movement should be taken as seriously in the 1970s as the Christian Stewardship movement had been in the 1960s,

I knew what he was talking about. He had in mind, I think, more than the film which the Reverend Michael Harper showed to illustrate the charismatic movement of Pentecostalism, which involves many who remain regular members of the main churches. At the Church Leaders' Conference I saw more clearly than ever before that what Christianity needs is a new Pentecost, giving knowledge where there is now confusion, confidence where there is now doubt, and joy where there is now despair – and, as the source of all this, giving a new disclosure of the truth. The raising of more money to prop up the churches' present organization – for that is what 'Christian Stewardship' has usually amounted to – will scarcely be the answer to the religious crisis.

I was the more ready to accept this semi-Pentecostal experience in Birmingham because the conference thoroughly and repeatedly acknowledged that God is to be found 'in the happenings of our time' (as Derrick Greeves had put it), in the problems themselves rather than in any easy answers (as David Jenkins hammered home). Despite the severe limitations of time and ability, no problem was deliberately shirked.

Paul Oestreicher wrote in *The Times*: 'Asked whether non-Catholics might before too long be allowed to receive Communion in his church, Cardinal Heenan replied that he could only conceive of that in the most exceptional circumstances. Maybe in a concentration camp. That provoked what was certainly the conference's wittiest retort from that meeting's chairman, Canon Bernard Pawley of St Paul's Cathedral, who deeply knows and deeply loves the Roman Catholic Church: "It seems, then, that we should pray for a multiplication of concentration camps." Perhaps it was also one of the conference's profoundest remarks. For it may well be true that the church will only be set free to proclaim a new humanity in Christ when it enters fully into the sufferings of the world. In the prison camps of Rhodesia and Siberia, in the police cellars of Brazil and Greece, there are no vested ecclesiastical interests to be protected. No silver chalices, but tin cups of cold water. One humanity and the freedom to share forgiveness.

'That world was never far from Birmingham. The Archbishop of York was able to tell his friends that he had never known how many people did not know how to spell "bastard" until he offered to take in a family of Ugandan Asians. And so 500 more or less humble Christians talked and prayed together ... knowing only too well how costly it would be to put those words into action ... The talk was of prayer and its centrality, of politics and its inescapability, of social change and its human consequences, of our rape of the earth and the need to live less greedily ... Nor was the continuing need for Christian unity forgotten or despaired of. No longer now just ecclesiastical mergers but churches ready to die themselves in order that they might live in a new, almost unrecognizable, world of scientific and ecological revolution, to live in and through Christ for and with that world.'

There was no emotional drama at Birmingham. No superstar of the pulpit emerged, although there was universal admiration for the liveliness (and content) of the Archbishop of Canterbury's address to the conference and about 12,000 other Christians gathered by the Birmingham Council of Christian Churches from over the West Midlands for a rally in Cannon Hill Park during the chilly afternoon of Sunday 17 September; the text was that Jesus wept over the city. The opening and closing services of the conference were restrained, although far less conservative than the worship had been at Nottingham 1964. Members of the conference read from the Bible or from modern writings, twentieth-century hymns were sung, recorded classical music was played, there was silence (ten minutes on the first evening, before 'free' prayer). The only new symbolic actions which the conference allowed itself were to distribute small loaves of brown bread ('not eucharistic', it had to be explained) to the 12,000 on Sunday afternoon; and, in the quiet of the George Cadbury Hall at the end, to sign book-markers which each member was asked to give to his or her neighbour as a souvenir of friendship.

In the conference's worship the problematic world was never forgotten, and the last words were a poem by Miroslav Holub, read by the Reverend Caryl Micklem who had devised the closing service:

Go and open the door.
Maybe outside there's
a tree, or a wood,
a garden,
or a magic city ...
If there's a fog
it will clear ...
At least
there'll be
a draught.

But for all this realism and restraint, the conference felt the movement of the Holy Spirit. To say this is to agree with *Upside* that 'our experience together has, we hope, thrown into disrepute for all time outdated methods of education and authoritarian leadership'. But to say this is not to claim any high status for the documents which resulted. It had never been intended that prolonged attention would be demanded for the always tedious process of drafting documents, but one problem increased by the conference's chosen method of informal group-discussion rather than plenary debate was the problem of making the documents worthy of the occasion – and worth passing on to the churches which had produced the money and released the time. To the end, one commission insisted on producing a complicated chart showing the circular course of its own theological discussion, rather than any report which might throw clear light for the average reader on the question this commission had been asked, 'Who is Christ for men today?' The problem of how to combine the warmth generated by group dynamics with careful arguments which would impress somebody who had not enjoyed the group's experience was one which thoughtful members of the conference spotted, and which would have to be solved if anything like the method developed by Birmingham 1972 was to be used in the decision-making bodies of the churches or of the nation.

The Church Leaders' Conference is therefore never likely to be regarded as infallible. Its experience of the Holy Spirit was of a different nature. It was the experience of an ecumenical encounter leading to a richer understanding; the experience of learning through meeting.

The many tensions, public and private, turned out to be tolerable because a spirit of charity prevailed and resulted in the desire to learn. The Steering Committee patiently revised the programme, with the result that the passengers were allowed to steer. Thus reassured, few of the passengers abandoned the ship in mid-voyage; and those who reached port did so wearily but in a happiness which impressed hardened conference-goers. The meetings of the commissions and their sub-groups, although not all equally successful, were in the main greatly enjoyed. Many friendships were formed which will strengthen the churches' renewal and reunion. The plenary sessions, originally resentful, were towards the end swept by frequent laughter – and people were laughing at the same things. A deep unity of spirit was the foundation of the conference's success, which was more substantial than had been expected either in the planning or in the early stages. It gave hope that the hard questions of theology, administration and politics which were raised at the conference would be tackled with a new energy.

To a social scientist, it was group-work in a learning experience: leading not from the front but from the middle. To a theologian, it was the fellowship of the Holy Spirit: the leading of the Lord, the giver of life. To a student of recent history, it was the articulation of themes previously half-heard. To a prophet, it may have been a turning to the future.

2

The Laymen and the Cardinal

The Emerging Future

The Christian laymen who were the first two lecturers expected an affluent future for Britain. First, however, both reminded the conference that some of the British churches' own malaise was due to the depression in the society around them. The English Sickness had replaced *Pax Britannica.*

Peter Walker recalled that at school in 1945 'I was being taught history on the basis of how Britain had become the greatest power in the world. We had just defeated Germany and Japan. Now I find myself a member of the Cabinet with that power, measured in military or economic terms, unimportant compared with other great powers, and the British Empire ended. Indeed there have been recent times when this country has been greatly in debt to the very nations we defeated in 1945.'

'Now we are no longer at the centre of the world ... How to describe the effect of all this on us I do not know,' Sir William Armstrong said. 'I have seen nostalgia and chagrin in the old, bewilderment in the middle aged, and impatient incomprehension in the young. An enormous natural complacency has been shattered.'

But both men from the centre of political knowledge and power embodied an assurance that, despite its present bewilderment, post-imperial Britain was moving into a good future. Leadership in such a time was, Peter Walker said, 'a very exciting challenge, perhaps more exciting than at any other time'. (Evidently he was not so ashamed as some churchmen present to be a leader.) One change to which he drew attention was the 'disappearance of the strongly held dogmas of the latter part of the nineteenth century'. The dogmas both of *laissez-faire* capitalism and of Marxism were becoming 'matters of historical interest only'.

The criticisms of capitalism offered by this leading Conservative politician aroused special interest. 'One has to change the whole employer/employee concept'; a new partnership has to develop despite 'the clash of industrial relations today' – just as a new relationship between the proprietor and the manager has to be worked out. And 'I believe another unacceptable feature of capitalism is the degree to which it can unreasonably exploit the resources of the world or fail to speedily remedy the poverty that exists.' Although the British public is not yet sufficiently aware of the problems of the poor nations, 'in a much smaller world it is inconceivable that this world can reach a position of peace and contentment when the gap continues to widen'.

Another change is that 'this is almost certainly the first period in history where those in their twenties and early thirties are better educated than the majority of people in their fifties and sixties'. But Peter Walker recalled how 'I appointed a twenty-six-year-old to be the chairman of a new town and I received a little note back from No. 10 Downing Street (not from the Prime Minister himself, but from his office) and they said very simply "we presume this is a typing error and you meant sixty-two".' He also claimed that 'my generation looks upon jumping on a plane to go to New York, Africa or Asia as part of a pretty regular routine'. If this aroused the disbelief of some of the church leaders, others in subsequent lectures or discussions showed that they, too, could readily produce anecdotes from their globe-trotting.

'Technology will enable more people to spend far less time applying their lives to uninteresting routines in very ugly surroundings,' Peter Walker prophesied. 'Do not expect that those leaving our schools and universities in the coming decade are going to accept for themselves a life where they go into a factory or office in boring routines from nine to five!' But technology can also enable some of the ideals of the younger generation to be translated into practice. In a global context, already 'we have a commercial position which could enable us to do far more in closing this gap between rich and poor'; and within Britain already Mr Walker's own Department of the Environment, with a staff of 78,000 and a budget of £3,000 million a year, has powers over land use, planning, transport and all the anti-pollution agencies in the country. He mentioned a recent visit to Stoke-on-Trent, 'which has more tip heaps and derelict land than any city in Europe . . . and one knew that in ten years all of those 7,000 acres would be parkland, marinas and areas of elegance and good living'.

Sir William Armstrong added his observations as one who had spent his time since 1945 'at the centre of the government machine'. He recalled: 'In 1945 the Labour Government, with a good deal of war-time planning behind them, launched us into a social revolution on a vast scale. Apart from the necessary clearing up of the aftermath of war, they had three main planks: the management of the economy to guarantee full employment; the taking into public ownership and control of the basic industries, together with the control of the use of land; and the introduction of what has come to be called the Welfare State, specifically the setting up of a comprehensive free health service and a universal system of social security benefits. There has not, so far as I know, been anything quite like it in our history, either for its scale or for its consequences for the future. Subsequent governments of either side have done very little to alter the pattern laid down in those first post-war years.'

Sir William acknowledged that 'it is difficult now to remember the enthusiasm with which all this was greeted'. Although the lot of the common people has 'improved enormously' since the war from a material standpoint ('we drink more tea and beer, and watch and play more games, than any other nation'), some disillusion has set in.

'Successive governments have not been able to live up completely to their promises: unemployment has risen, inflation continues, economic growth continues to elude us,' Sir William said. 'This is giving rise to a disbelief in the power of governments, an angry frustration with the large organizations which the government has created, a cynicism about politics, and a search for forms of direct action. Secondly, people are beginning to realize that the government is not a universal provider with a bottomless purse, but only themselves under another name: and those who see themselves as paying taxes for someone else's benefit are beginning to want governments that will reduce taxes, or failing that, to seek ways and means of avoiding paying taxes themselves. Thirdly, a man's sense of personal responsibility for his own material well-being and that of his family, and the notion that went with it that you can only improve your standard of living by working for it, are being seriously undermined.'

Sir William added a very sombre warning. 'The foundation of it all is becoming dangerously thin: the work we do, the wealth we create, is not increasing anything like as fast as it would have to if we are all going to go on living as well as we do, let alone any better. In one way or another, hard times are coming again.'

But after this warning, the Head of the Civil Service went on to promises. 'I am quite sure that in the long run we shall get over our natural bewilderment and find ways of putting the emphasis back on productivity.' And he made it clear that he agreed with Peter Walker that this productivity would be possible without drudgery. 'It seems likely that before long the five day working week will become a four day one. Perhaps we may go even further and allow people to settle their own work-times ... with no universal day off.'

Sir William looked forward to a day when there would be 'so much more time away from bread-winning that people will be increasingly interested in the quality of life where they are living it and leisure, just because there will be so much of it, will increasingly become used for activities which are better done voluntarily. So we may get back to a time when husbands and wives, and fathers and children, see and live with each other all day for days on end.' To help fill this leisure, 'both television and radio will eventually be available twenty-four hours of every day and night' and 'automatic home recording will be cheap and universal, while videotape cassettes and sound cassettes will be as plentiful as paperbacks.' Another way of occupying the coming age of leisure was suggested by 'the likely advent of universal, safe contraception'.

What of the Church?

Whether hard times were coming, or an age of leisure, or both, these laymen seemed uncertain about the role of the church in the future.

Peter Walker, himself an Anglican churchgoer, hinted at some impatience with much of the church's routine. He spoke of a statesman he had known, who had meditated for an hour each day. He remarked: 'If the majority of clergy for that hour each day asked themselves to what extent they have applied their abilities, enthusiasms and energy to creating the type of world and the type of life they consider Christianity is all about, and subjected themselves to that brutal daily examination over the course of an hour, I do wonder to what extent they might not take new attitudes, develop new practices and apply their time and efforts in differing ways. There are sections of activity in the church that I think are immensely encouraging; like the activites of the industrial chaplains. I have long admired the great work of the Catholic Housing Association. But there is an immense sphere where active Christian purpose needs to be applied ...'

As befitted Britain's top civil servant, Sir William Armstrong was more specific. He wanted to see Christians more active in an increasingly mobile society – 'not earnest placard carriers, but Christians who are themselves working or playing or watching with the others'. He threw out one idea for a Religious Broadcasting Corporation, 'broadcasting certainly in sound and eventually in vision too, all day, every day'; and another for more sex education of other people's children by Christian fathers and mothers – 'I am thinking of what I believe lay behind many of the initiation ceremonies of primitive tribes.'

But he was unclear as to the base from which such operations might be conducted. He recalled how, after a boyhood in the Salvation Army in which his parents served, he had become a 'conscientious agnostic' by the time he had won his way to Oxford. He had later recovered some faith, and had enjoyed taking charge of the teaching of the children in Sanderstead Congregational Church: 'I have little doubt that it was watching my children grow from babyhood to childhood, and wondering what to tell them about life and death and religion, that brought me back.' But he had moved to live in the centre of London, 'and since then, for the last nine years, I have never been to an ordinary Sunday service in any church'.

Sir William offered no analysis of his withdrawal, simply saying about his failure to find a church that 'suited' him: 'I haven't tried very hard.' He had, it appeared, grown thoroughly bored. Like millions of other laymen, Sunday after Sunday he voted with his feet. And he added this brief plea about Christian doctrine. 'I would dearly love the leaders of the church to say clearly and unequivocally how much of the traditional Christian story and inherited doctrine they believe, how much they interpret away, how much they have mental reservations about, and how much they simply reject. I have tried to do this for myself and have arrived at a set of propositions which seem to me both to satisfy my intellect and to preserve my faith in Christ – but I do not have the faintest idea whether there is any church on earth that would accept me as a Christian. It would be nice to know: but I do not think that I should presume to ask for it.'

The Cardinal Speaks

How would the spokesmen of the churches respond?

The contrast in tone between these two laymen and Cardinal John Heenan, Archbishop of Westminster, was emphasized in some of the first sentences in his lecture. The laymen had seemed eager to meet the church leaders. The Cardinal said: 'Although in no way cynical, I have to confess that I am never over-confident of hearing God's voice at conferences – neither here today nor, for example, next month at the meeting of our Bishops' Conference in Westminster. God can and does use councils, synods and conferences as channels of his grace, but it has so far been my experience that God's voice is more likely to be heard in our daily prayer or while we are about our daily work.' And in contrast with the laymen who had been eager to talk about the future, the Cardinal was ironic. 'Today's church is more difficult to describe than tomorrow's. What the church will then be like is literally anyone's guess. It is easy to speak of tomorrow because until tomorrow comes nobody can contradict.'

Surveying the Roman Catholic Church today, the Cardinal adopted a tone similar to the one in which the laymen had spoken about post-imperial Britain's economic problems. 'The church of 1972 presents an aspect in many respects different from the church of 1962,' he said. 'The question we are going to ask ourselves is to what extent these changes have been for the better. The answer will depend on the outlook of the individual Catholic.'

'For many – perhaps for most – the second Vatican Council has been a triumph for the Holy Spirit,' the Cardinal explained. 'The church, *semper reformanda*, has been reformed. The old superior attitudes have gone. Complacency has been disturbed and false spiritual security undermined. That is one view. Other Catholics deplore much of what the Council has done. Solid doctrine, they say, has been displaced in favour of theological opinions. The old certainties and pieties have been destroyed. Authority, the greatest attraction of the Church of Rome, has been eroded from within. This view is sometimes shared by those outside the Roman obedience. An Anglican layman said to me a few days ago: "I know it sounds absurd coming from a church which boasts of accepting all shades of opinion to say so, but many of us Anglicans did rather rely on you people to uphold standards of faith and morals in these permissive times."'

'Between extremes there is the main body of unemotional Catholics,' the Cardinal added. 'They do not write letters to the press. They distrust controversialists and put their faith in Christ's promise that his church will never fail. These people take for granted that the second Vatican Council was guided by God as surely as the first. This kind of Catholic had small difficulty in accepting papal infallibility from the first Vatican Council and no more difficulty in taking ecumenism and liturgical reform from the second.'

As he gave 'one man's impression of what the Catholic Church looks like in the aftermath of the Council', Cardinal Heenan stressed the hesitations of 'ordinary Catholics'. The great majority, he reported, were anxious to be friendly with non-Catholics but not to worship in their churches, and 'they have no interest in what we call the ecumenical dialogue'. Most were, he said, 'unreservedly grateful for the English Mass', but there seemed to be reservations here, too – about the 'frequently unmelodious translations' and 'bobbing-up-and-down'. The Cardinal confessed that the bishops in the Council had failed to foresee 'that Latin would virtually disappear from Catholic churches'.

He welcomed some of the results of recent discussion. 'In preconciliar days a convert would talk of making his submission to Rome. Ecumenical Catholics no longer think – much less talk – of submission. It is of the essence of true ecumenism to recognize that much of what divided Christendom was a difference of emphasis or even of semantics. Who, for example, would have thought ten years ago that Anglicans and Roman Catholics could reach any sort of agreement on the eucharist?' He also recognized that 'a reaction against the manner of exercising authority in the Catholic Church was clearly due. Bishops, superiors and, in lesser degree, parish priests could rule dioceses, communities or parishes in despotic fashion.'

But the Cardinal saw great dangers in what he called 'the cult of talk' – and he devoted the main part of his lecture to these dangers, rather than to any vision of the future.

'Consultation is excellent and necessary provided discussion is not allowed to inhibit action,' he said. 'When we wish to avoid action the venerable English custom is to appoint a committee. In the ecclesiastical world a new custom has arisen. Now, whenever the need for urgent action is admitted, a committee (usually called a commission) is formed or a conference is arranged. Clergy – and especially bishops – can spend a major part of their time at meetings. There are parish councils, deanery councils, diocesan councils of administration, schools commissions, liturgical commissions, ecumenical commissions, senates of priests and pastoral councils. There are frequent meetings of the hierarchy and of national commissions for education, seminaries, theology, the laity, liturgy, justice and peace, social welfare, religious life and foreign missions. All of these commissions have their quota of bishops and priests. Not to be outdone by the local church, the Holy See regularly summons bishops from the six continents to Rome for international commissions, conferences and synods.'

This is a style of life to which activists such as Peter Walker and Sir William Armstrong are well accustomed in the secular sphere. But it is a new style for the Roman Catholic Church, and Cardinal Heenan evidently found it difficult to believe that a bishop or priest could learn much in this way – or that the majority of the laity should, or could, subscribe to the new fashion of free participation. When answering a question informally, he created a minor sensation by observing that some laymen preferred conferences while others liked yachting.

Catholics, he pointed out in his lecture, 'are bound to go to Mass on Sundays and Holy Days. If the obligation were removed I am sure that we would not retain our crowded churches for long. When fish on Friday became optional, few continued the practice of Friday abstinence. It is a fact of life that most of us are not disposed to do what is good for us unless it is made a matter of duty.' He also observed that 'the idea of sharing responsibility with the clergy is excellent, but most laity still prefer to leave the priests to run the parish. The laity are free not to accept responsibility for administration and the vast majority exercise that freedom. Clergy are less free. They are now expected to spend a great deal of time sharing responsibility. Some wear themselves out discussing how this is to be done and lose their appetite for the ordinary pastoral round' – to the laity's disappointment, for 'the old saying remains true that a house-going priest makes a churchgoing people'.

Cardinal Heenan expressed great concern about other effects of 'the cult of talk'. After the solemn pronouncement by Pope Paul about birth control, 'a number of priests and laymen defied the Pope. Such behaviour was unprecedented in the well-disciplined church of the twentieth century and the church has not recovered and may never fully recover from the shock . . . I think it likely that many who have left the priesthood or the religious life would still be with us if they had not dissipated their zeal in endless talking. Nobody who has taken up the cross should lay it down.'

He turned to the theological crisis. 'Ecumenism', he said, 'will obviously have its effect on theological trends in all religions. That, indeed, is one of the primary objects of ecumenism. It has already altered Catholic thinking but it may bring another kind of development. Although for ecumenical reasons the word heretic is never used today, heretics still exist. The chief heresy is what we used to call modernism. In dealing with it the methods of Pope Pius X would no longer be possible or desirable, but I think that modernism is returning, and that it will re-appear as the chief threat to the church of tomorrow. Since authority and every kind of establishment have become universally unpopular, the climate was never more favourable for a renewed attack on the authority of God and the *magisterium* of his church.

'The Resurrection, the Blessed Trinity, the immortality of the soul, the sacraments, the Sacrifice of the Mass, the indissolubility of marriage, the right to the life of the unborn, the senile and the incurably sick – all these doctrines taken for granted by Catholics until now are likely to be attacked from within the church of tomorrow. According to press reports this year's Conference of Modern Churchmen decided to offer membership to some Catholics. That would have been unthinkable in the church of yesterday, but it is an indication of the problems which the church of tomorrow may be facing. Modernism is already showing its face in the current writing of popular theologians of whom some have clearly ceased to believe that Christ is truly God.'

Cardinal Heenan ended, however, on a somewhat more cheerful note – one which Bishop Butler later amplified (see Appendix A in this book). 'The churches of tomorrow will, I believe, grow closer together,' the Cardinal said. 'In God's good time we shall talk not of the churches but of one church. This, at least, seems certain – Christians will never return to the old rivalries and enmities. As religious belief declines in the West they will unite in an evangelical spirit to preach Christ to their brethren and lead them to the One Holy Catholic and Apostolic Church.'

An experienced journalist present considered this the best speech of the conference, judging it as oratory; and in many – probably most – Christian assemblies its contents would have seemed moving and impressive. Its repeated notes of worry and weariness and in particular its dismay over the heresies of popular theologians, would have aroused fellow-feelings in circles far beyond the Roman Catholic Church. But Margaret Duggan reported in the (Anglican) *Church Times* the conference's unhappy reactions to the Cardinal's visit. 'He came from the outside world, with no experience of the warm cohesion that had already started to grow. And it wasn't just what he said, but the way he said it ... While he had expressed the traditionally-held views of quite a few of the Roman episcopate there, many of the Roman Catholic representatives were in an agony of spirit; and the wave of sympathy which swept round them was one of the most memorable phenomena of the conference. One Roman priest told me gratefully that he was immediately carried off to the bar by two of his friends – both Anglican bishops – and fortified with large whiskies until he had recovered. At least two others had to go for a lonely walk before they could face other members of the conference.'

The conference reacted in this way because the basic question left in the air by Cardinal Heenan's lecture was whether the church he described so candidly, and served with such devotion, would have much of a place in the future as (in his own words) 'religious belief declines in the West'. Could it do convincingly what Sir William Armstrong most wanted – 'both to satisfy my intellect and to preserve my faith in Christ'? Church leaders present privately criticized Sir William for failing to grasp the idea of loyalty to the church as the body of Christ. But could the church of Cardinal Heenan's lecture represent Christ to the emerging future? This remained a question for which large whiskies could find no answer.

3

Two Christianities?

Two Psychologies

In the ecumenical movement it has often been said that Christians agree fundamentally. For example, a passage from a report adopted by the 1964 Faith and Order Conference was read during the opening worship at this 1972 Church Leaders' Conference. 'The churches must agree in their fundamental faith if they are to unite ... Can we be sure that we all have the same faith in the same Christ? Our answer is: yes.' But by the middle of this conference it seemed a real question whether Christianity can nowadays be more than a federation of faiths. The divisions between the denominations were thought by most members to be major obstacles to the Christian mission in the modern world, but to be less significant than the fundamental cleavages of theological conviction.

Apparently a basic split was revealed between two psychologies. These psychologies support not only the Christian lives of practical men such as Sir William Armstrong and Cardinal Heenan, but also considered theologies. On the one hand, there is a psychology of openness, supporting a theology of adventure. God cannot be known fully, but fragments of his activity can be glimpsed and joined from time to time as people open themselves to the impact of fresh experiences and new problems. On the other hand, there is a psychology of reverence and humble study, supporting a doctrinal system. God cannot be obeyed perfectly, but the essence of his nature can be seen through his self-revelation enshrined in the Bible and in the great tradition of the church. Each psychology seemed to its adherents within this conference to be the main source of vitality for Christians in the contemporary crisis, and each theology seemed to its supporters to be the best possible statement of truth.

During this conference it became apparent that members of the same denomination could differ profoundly in psychology and theology. We have always expected this of Anglicans; but we saw that the same is now true of Roman Catholics, of Baptists, and of all the churches. In each denomination radicals and conservatives who were profoundly suspicious of each other managed somehow to put up with each other as bedfellows. Uniformity became finally inconceivable. An era of 'theological pluralism' was announced – by some with joy, by others with regret that either radicalism (to Cardinal Heenan, modernism) or orthodoxy could not yet prevail completely. Conservative church leaders were told from many sources that they must learn to live with questions – if not their own, then other people's. Rebels against the past were also told that they must learn to live with faith – if not their own, then the conservatives'. They had all heard such things before; but day after day in this conference, pluralism was hammered home. It was not easy to be told such things; but at least the seriousness of the psychological and theological tensions gave perspective to the inherited debates about the best form of church government. 'What kind of God?' seemed to matter more than 'what kind of bishop?'. And when fundamentalism and modernism were known to co-exist within a single denomination, the impossibility of uniting that denomination with any other became more and more ridiculous.

The Crisis of Faith

The lecture by Dr Ian Ramsey, Bishop of Durham and formerly Nolloth Professor of the Philosophy of the Christian Religion, Oxford, was his first major engagement since a heart attack some months before, and his last major statement before his death less than four weeks later. It was a lecture which vigorously summed up his whole life's work.

'For long years,' Dr Ramsey recalled, 'theology was supposed to participate in the givenness of God himself. Its words were supposedly authenticated and guaranteed by the revelation they expressed. In that sense theology was a part of the revelation of God – so that in a literal, direct sense there were revealed truths. Revelation not only referred to an activity of God in Christ; it referred to particular God-given propositions as well. God did not only act, he spoke; he not only spoke, he dictated. On this view, it is not surprising that theology should seek to control and prescribe the conclusions in every other subject while being itself unaffected by discoveries about the world. Determinative of other knowledge, it was a purveyor of truths which all other studies must accept.'

This was, the Bishop noted, a generally accepted view as recently as a century ago. Faced with the challenge of new knowledge – for example, the challenge of geology to Genesis – 'men became negative not to say neurotic, insensitive not to say incensed, in the defence of the *status quo*. I have often wished that a century ago we had the mass-media of today which, whatever be their defects, would at least have ensured that in every home there was a hearing on all sides. True, the nineteenth century would have been to many even more shattering than it was; but there could not have been the same self-confidence and hollow victories. As we face the crisis of our own time, the reaction of our predecessors to the crisis of a past age is a terrible warning. Not only did they fail to face up squarely to searching issues; their side-stepping merely postponed until today the crisis which should have been faced yesterday.'

But Dr Ramsey was almost as critical of the old 'liberals' in religion as he was of the conservatives. 'I will not be arguing for a liberalism of an outdated brand,' he said. 'The older liberals were men of broad views and great integrity, and on the whole they saw the problems, and asked the right questions, at a time when a question mark was thought to be almost a symbol of blasphemy. But their answers tended to be shallow and superficial, largely because with no sense of the variegations of language they took science as definitive, so that not surprisingly a sense of mystery, not to mention the distinctiveness of the Christian faith, seemed to evaporate and disappear.'

And, if he attacked the mistakes of the nineteenth century, Dr Ramsey was no less outspoken about our generation's failures.

'For too long we have failed to come to grips with this issue,' he declared. 'Historical studies over the last century and a half have made it plain that theology cannot have a monolithic and self-guaranteed character; that there is no precision-built theology to be prescriptive. It only gained this appearance in the past by Christians taking cognizance of only a partial selection of the relevant facts, with different Christians taking different selections and making sure they never met each other. Critical historical studies make it impossible to hold, for instance, that there is but one view of the Christian ministry which itself contains the whole truth; that alternative views are just verbiage. Again, the idea that doctrinal controversy yields clear unambiguous views of (say) Christological or Trinitarian truth can hardly be sustained ... It is high time that theology as she is preached and theology as she is practised in liturgies listened to theology as she is taught. A Nelson's eye attitude has run through preaching and liturgy for far too long.'

Dr Ramsey stressed the difficulty of 'reading off God's purposes in nature and history – a point which lies behind John Wisdom's famous remark: "The existence of God is not an experimental issue in the way it was."' He quoted from the report of the inquiry into religious education which he had led, *The Fourth R*: 'On the one hand there was the theological view that God controlled the events of nature – rain or sunshine. Natural calamities were viewed as punishment, national prosperity as reward. God was directly involved alike in man's prosperity as in his failures. Further, it was God who gave men the victory in battles between nations. Yet for some four hundred years men have been developing very different interpretations of nature, human nature, and history. The new ways of talking about the world, about human nature, about history, not only seem never to need the concept of God, but often seem to be in head-on collision with all the ways of talking traditional to the theologian.'

The challenge of the new understanding to the traditional ways of teaching the Christian religion was stated candidly. 'It it all too easy to misread the Bible in such a way as to conclude that God uses men as mere mouth-pieces,' the Bishop confessed. 'Unless we are either very unsophisticated or very sophisticated, passages in the Bible which use the word "God" as the subject of a sentence are hazardous in the extreme: for they read as if God had been observed to say and to do precisely what is there described. They conceal the fact that the words are the writer's interpretation of a situation, not his reporting of observable features as news of the world and God ... I am bound to ask whether the situation has been helped by a traditional catechism which, however excellent as a syllabus, is absolutely disastrous when indicative of a method, since it presupposes a way of learning which, of all others, is least likely to help a pupil to make what is learned part of themselves.'

'Where in fact do we look for an approach to the Bible and doctrine which has learned from the problems, mistakes and difficulties of the last century and a half?' Dr Ramsey asked. 'Does a broad common intention and outlook unite minister and clergy on the one hand and teachers on the other? Are we over stocked with theologically educated, or even just theologically well-informed, laymen? I am not here apportioning blame; I am simply recognizing a feature to which we must not be blind if we are ever to emerge from our present crisis on the right side.'

Dr Ramsey was also frank about the consequences for the church's moral reasoning. 'Nowhere have the collisions and tensions emerged with more unmistakable force and clarity than in the area of human nature and human behaviour, not least because of the comparatively recent developments in psychology and the behavioural sciences generally. At one time, sin and wrongdoing seemed to be clear and unambiguous. But not only developments in psychology, more lately developments in the biological and medical sciences, and in endocrinology in particular, have led to an acknowledgment of new factors which must be reckoned with when we appraise human behaviour. Glandular secretions and biochemical imbalance are of undeniable importance in any full understanding of human behaviour; it may not always be John himself but his testosterone which is to be blamed for John's sexual irregularities. It was once supposed that, left alone in the isolation of a prison cell, a person would come to his senses, be brought to penitence, and all would be well. What so often happens is that when judgments such as this are now rejected on empirical grounds, the rejection is taken to be a rejection of Christian theology; and so it would be – and will be – if this is all Christian theology has to say.'

Dr Ramsey then outlined the alternative approach: *Christian empiricism*. Since *empirical* is defined by the Oxford Dictionary as 'based on, or guided by, the results of observation and experiment only', any plea for a Christian variety of this approach implies a defence of religious belief and language.

'There is no single brand of reliable reasoning,' the Bishop said. 'At one time it was supposed that there was only one pattern of reliable argument. For Aristotle, this was given by the syllogism, especially when all syllogistic reasoning was supposed to be reducible to a single form. For Descartes, the only brand of reliable reasoning was mathematics, and philosophy itself had to conform to that pattern. For the positivists, whether of the nineteenth century or our own day, the ideal was the language of the experimental sciences. But no one any longer supposes that reliable reasoning is restricted to a single pattern of argument, nor that there must be only one explanation of a particular state of affairs. On the contrary, it is recognized that there are many different patterns of reliable reasoning, e.g. in mathematics, history, poetry, theology; and that there can be a logical multiplicity of explanations – points sometimes encapsulated in the slogan "Every assertion has its own logic."'

'In order to see what is being talked about,' the Bishop explained, 'we must consider words in the context of sentences, themselves in the context of discourse, which itself is given its full concrete situational setting. Personal situations may well provide helpful parallels to those situations in which religious language is grounded, and here the interests of the empiricist and those of existentialist can come close to each other.'

Dr Ramsey recalled from Cambridge days his own struggle to find a way of doing theology in this intellectual climate. 'It was when I had asked myself such questions in a youthfulness surrounded by logical positivists and challenged at every point to elucidate the meaningfulness of religious discourse, that I came to see that such discourse cannot do without alluding to the facts and features of the world around us, yet cannot be satisfied with such an empirical cashing alone. It must appeal to empirical criteria *and more*: but not more such criteria, or else there is no transcendence; nor to similar criteria but in another world, for that is to buy sense and reference at the cost of intelligibility. Faced by this predicament, I came to talk of *disclosure* as that by which the transcendent makes itself known in and through things spatial and temporal, whether subjectively as that in ourselves which is more than our observable behaviour, or objectively as that which we speak of in terms of the word of God. As we look around us, some so-called "facts" are there to be looked at – in the case of persons, eyes, ears, hair and skin; but some other facts declare themselves, make themselves known to us, they capture our attention or disclose themselves, and that is how we recognize persons, personal activity, spirit.

'In short,' Dr Ramsey declared, 'theology and all religious claims, Christian or any other, in the end appeal to disclosures, moments of vision, flashes of insight, though those phrases conceal the point that a disclosure may not be at all spectacular, but rather possess the impressiveness and growing significance of a silence. Hence the two metaphors – "the ice breaks" (a spectacular discontinuity) and "the light dawns" (a gradual awakening). Perhaps I should add that I speak of revelation when the disclosure occurs in a Christian context. It is in such situations of vision and disclosure – where a flat, impersonal, narrowly empirical situation takes on depth and another dimension – that theology arises. Theology trades in models and metaphors each of which occurs within, and arises from a particular disclosure situation, and each of which licenses discourse by which we can be articulate about what the disclosure discloses. So theology becomes a complex interweaving of different strands of discourse, each proceeding from different models, and each at different points and in different ways being qualified so as to indicate their disclosure basis. For all the strands are attempting to be articulate in one way or another about a vision.'

Dr Ramsey then outlined the task of the church as he saw it. 'We must find ways and means of creating, for our contemporaries as for ourselves, moments of vision and disclosure. For without these there is no cash value to be given to anything we say or do. Without such occasions of insight there can be no foothold for religious discourse in general, or for the Christian faith in particular. Our contemporaries will then rightly conclude that Christian institutions are at best no more than phenomena with an impressive past and little future, catering for those who happen to like the kind of social behaviour to be found in our synods and assemblies, our churches and chapels, our schoolrooms and parish halls. Our primary and urgent need, on which all else depends, is to make possible occasions when our society could re-discover a sense of the sublime. Mary Warnock has recently written: "The concept of the sublime, which is not particularly widely discussed at the present time, is all the same of the greatest importance. When many people were religious they had the sublime, to some extent, tamed, and available to them on Sundays. But now most of them have not, and without it their lives may suddenly seem too banal and too completely intelligible to be worth living. Their imaginations are starved by the well-explored material limits of their lives, because one can't separate the notion of the sublime from that of the limitless or infinite."

'I see a great significance at this point in the present popularity of festivals,' the Bishop added. 'Festivals provide the means by which, today, the haunting vision can be recreated around key ideas, symbols, which are sufficiently open-textured to transmit a true power, the power of inspiration from which discourse can be derived. Further, as artists and technicians, composers and players, give form and context to the ideas and symbols, people mingle together and discuss them, and thus begin to lay the foundation for the frameworks, the cathedrals of ideas and corporate action, in which power can and must be expressed so that a reasonable religion can influence social change and development ... Basically a prayer should be discourse apt to the evoking of a disclosure, consistent and coherent with our ideas of God, man and the world, and linked effectively with some practical action ... I recall how in Canada a barbecue stove, a secular symbol of fellowship and joy in the universe, became that in which incense was burnt and over which were offered to God the prayers of the congregation. On some other occasion bread and wine could easily have taken the place of steak and baked potatoes.'

Dr Ramsey also called for the formation of more groups when religious leaders could meet laymen for serious discussions. He said: 'Such groups will recognize the need both for a classical theology which gives us the necessary professional background, and also for what has been called a "contextual" theology where believers develop the facility for latching on to the multiple discussion of a problem. Such a discussion not only aims at a creative decision; in reaching such a decision it discovers also new possibilities of theological articulation. It is in this contextual theology that there will be found the growing points of our faith and the intimations of a new culture, a culture Christian, scientific, technological and humane ... I cannot exaggerate the necessity for trans-disciplinary groups, nor their significance, nor their theological and educational value, any more than their novelty and difficulty.' In later discussions he illustrated the value of such groups from the work of recent groups studying the ethics of abortion and euthanasia. In these studies no single factor – such as the inviolable foetus – had been isolated. Everything had been taken together. But the groups had found some light, for 'the purpose of the group, so far as human nature allows, is to enable a new disclosure'.

Finally, Dr Ramsey outlined the consequences for church leadership. 'We do not give a lead – though those who ask us for one often suppose we do – by reiterating conclusions which those around us wish to hear or wish to have without the trouble of reaching them. We give a lead only by displaying, in our utterances or otherwise, that which inspires us. "The power of God is the worship he inspires," said Whitehead.' Would this feed the sheep? The Bishop protested: 'The implication is sometimes that the only food suited to the sheep, and the only food they desire, is a prescribed diet of food devoid of roughage: which a moment's reflection will tell us is entirely unhealthy.'

The Struggle to be Human

More roughage in the conference's diet was provided in the lecture by Canon David Jenkins. It was entitled 'Faith in God and Man', but it ended with the question: 'How shall we give one another the courage to allow things to collapse to the point where we can discover what God is really doing, and then to be free enough to respond to him and to share it with him?'

David Jenkins drew on his study and teaching of philosophy in Oxford, and on his more recent experience as Director of the Humanum study project of the World Council of Churches, to stress how many problems now face not only the man who tries to believe but also the man who tries to be human. But he allowed some of those sympathetic with his off-the-cuff and near-the-bone criticisms to glimpse some fresh ways of trusting in God and therefore of believing that 'man has a future'. 'It is only in the arena of being and becoming human that there is any receiving of God and any responding to God,' he claimed – although 'this is not to say that God is simply the same thing as that arena', for in relation to man God is free and independent. 'But I think we can say more. I think we can dare to go on to say that becoming human is indeed "God's enterprise". Is this not the meaning of the Incarnation, the commitment of God himself to entering the human predicament as a human being? Because of this we hope, we dream, we struggle, we attempt to believe that the kingdom of God in its fulfilment will be the sharing of the fullness of being human through the sharing of the life of God ...

'This union of God and man by the creative, redemptive and fulfilling activity of God is always more than we can take. And the whole history of the church is a history of constantly being obliged to rediscover this truth. You have the history of the Christological heresies whereby it was never possible to keep the necessary dynamic balance of the mystery about God becoming human. You have the whole history of what I would call the imperialisms of the church, where again and again the church has supposed that she was to be identified with the kingdom of God. And you have also the whole history of Christian escapisms, whereby human beings were unable to be as down-to-earth and as much involved in history as the God whom Christians were supposed to follow.'

After this theological introduction, David Jenkins hit out at the 'really neurotic nature' of much Christian escapism – for example, the worry about whether or not the wine received in communion was fermented. 'Further, it is salutary to remember that in nearly all parts of the world at one time or another, and in one form or another, the very name of Jesus has been, and sometimes continues to be, associated with oppression and torture. Having recently returned from Australia I am reminded that one of the things that was done in the name of the gospel in Tasmania was to make sure there wasn't a race problem because all the blacks were killed off. I shall never forget the extremely moving paper written one night by an African pupil of mine which explained from the very depth of his being just what has been done by the missionaries to his country. I have recently returned from another part of the world where it is clear that the established church and the oppressive government go hand in hand ... God-talk and government-talk and establishment-talk have all tended to go together as a matter of fact. And if you look at the programme of this conference, the point may seem to be illustrated.

'Then there is the whole history of what I might call the "domination-dependence syndrome", which I am sure gave Freud so much material. It seems in so many of the practices and teachings and indeed liturgies of the churches that the worship of God goes with what I was taught in the army as promotion drill – which is down, crawl, salute, promote. Deeply uncomfortable questions about this matter of domination are being raised for us under the slogan-title of "women's liberation" but which is, of course, about human liberation. Reference to God as "he" has had immense effect on the way things are shaped. One of the questions that has been brought home to me more and more as I have had the misfortune to be involved in debates about abortion is "why should the moral tune by called by men?" '

In modern criticisms of the church, David Jenkins heard the voice of God. He struck an Old Testament note. 'God is constantly concerned to condemn his people, to make fools of his people, to break his people down in order that they be restored and renewed in the fullness of his service.' God is 'the disturber, and the problems which men and women face prevent them from settling down in anything less ultimate than the largeness of his love. These disturbances are real, they can undermine our whole identity, they will quite possibly blow up whole communities.' A growth of violence was to be expected. But 'we have to find a simplicity of living which will give us the freedom to face the complexity of living'. And his address made it clear that, for David Jenkins, the key to this simplicity of living is found in the symbol of 'Jesus the sufferer', who, crucified by the problems, is yet identical with 'God the disturber'. So our resources lie in the problems and in ourselves because that is where God is. He is in the struggles, the agonies and the hopes which the problems represent. 'He has committed himself to us as human beings, which is his whole enterprise for us ... He will not allow the human race as a whole to fall short of his kingdom ... Only God is sufficient for these things, but he comes to us through one another.'

Then David Jenkins sketched a programme for the church, subordinating its own welfare to the wider struggle to be human. This did not, he emphasized, mean reducing the gospel to secular humanism. 'If there is no God and there is no grace and there is nothing outside the universe then, if I may say so, for the sake of man join the communist party: don't go messing around with this bloke Jesus. If atheism and human aloneness are a reality, then there is a human way of responding to the human problem, and it is blasphemy to use that problem to keep some sort of vestigial religion.' But neither should the church's involvement in the human struggle mean leadership. 'We cannot lead; the question is how we can be set free to follow, to respond, to be part of the total response ... How can we dis-organize? How do we open the institutional church more and more to the experimental church, to the emergent church and to the no-church human struggle? ... How do we give one another the courage to fail at our enterprises and to say "no" to so many things? For to reorganize priorities and be open to new things, you must have time ... Full time on church affairs is a total waste of time.'

In the New Era of Science

That provocative address formed a sequel to Dr Ian Ramsey's. But the lecture by T. F. Torrance, Professor of Christian Dogmatics in Edinburgh, may have reminded hearers (or any who permitted themselves a fleeting thought about the Middle Ages) of the long-ago battles between Bishops of Durham and the invading Scots. At any rate, the contrast between Dr Ramsey and Dr Torrance was so obvious that the conference demanded that at a later plenary session the two should converse in public.

Dr Torrance submitted in writing a learned paper on 'The Church in the New Era of Scientific and Cosmological Change', but he delivered his lecture informally, and even more vigorously than his predecessors. His main thesis was that the 'progressive' fashions now dominant were in fact reactionary, because they belonged to a world-view being made obsolete by the latest science.

He came to the Church Leaders' Conference straight from an

international meeting of top scientists, and was not abashed when a professor of physics in his audience, W. R. Hindmarsh, said that he scarcely recognized his subject in the science being described. Whether or not they agreed with, or understood, his conclusions, most of the church leaders to whom he spoke in these two plenary sessions (and also in smaller meetings) were stimulated by the spectacle of a theologian who felt able to hold his own in the scientific era of the world, who freely expressed his contempt for the World Council of Churches, and who in passing rebuked one of the most formidable Roman Catholic teachers of the day, Karl Rahner, for having reduced theology to anthropology. When he advised the church leaders to sell their shirts (or skirts) for Jungmann's book on liturgical prayer – a book which, he added, was almost unobtainable in this country – they were impressed, if not persuaded. Most of his Roman Catholic hearers, who had patiently endured the previous lectures, were delighted by this Presbyterian.

Weaving together what was written and what was said, we may note first the insistence that 'we are in the midst of the biggest mutation in the structure of thought that has ever happened'. Dr Torrance compared this with a quake in the depths of the earth, which mattered far more than any superficial collapse or crack – and which might spread, tumbling mountains.

The old structure of Western thought had as its basis a dualism between heaven and earth, or between the absolute and the contingent, or between mind and matter, resulting in a series of theologies 'in which God remains eternally and immutably detached from the world and does not really interact with it'. In many modern theologies – or flights from theology – 'a wide gap opens up between an inert God who cannot be known in himself and the world of phenomena conceived as a closed continuum of cause and effect'. God gets like a ghost, and the world gets like a machine. But the gigantic revolution of thought associated with the name of Einstein had put an end to this dualism. The whole universe is now seen as a union of energy/matter, space/time: a reality which cannot be seen or touched or analysed by the old scientific methods or even described or perceived, but which is demonstrably there. The new humility of the scientist, who feels on the edge of a great leap forward of the mind, can be brought very close to the awe of the worshipper. In addition, there now exists a widespread revolt against the dehumanized technology and the ecological chaos produced by the use or misuse of the old science, so both in the intellectual and in the practical sphere the Christian church has a great chance – if it keeps its nerve.

But Dr Torrance severely criticized what he called the 'built-in obsolescence' of much of the church's current response to the age. While the advanced scientists bravely struggle to break free from conventional patterns of thought, the church seems to jump on every passing bandwaggon. So much of the church's involvement allows the obsolescent world to dictate its own terms. 'The medium is the message' and 'the world writes the agenda' were denounced as slogans, and the recent American proclamation of the death of God was analysed as no more than the acknowledgment that a phase of American-Christian culture had passed. The gospel, Dr Torrance insisted, cannot be communicated without a radical restructuring of the consciousness, in much the same way as Einsteinian physics is revolutionary.

In his written paper, Dr Torrance illustrated his plea for a 'scientific' theology by urging Roman Catholics to re-examine their traditions about the principate of St Peter, about the real presence of Christ in the Mass, and about the historical succession of bishops – all of which had been coloured by ideas coming in from new dead cultures. But in his speech, he directed his fire at his fellow-Protestants.

Protestantism, he declared, was now in danger of reducing Christianity to the 'pathological moralism' of the 'guilty intellectual'. Young ministers seemed to confuse treating a person therapeutically with leading that person to Jesus Christ, with the result that some Protestants had to rely on the Roman Catholic priest for pastoral care. The World Council of Churches seemed to believe that the church must act as a 'prestigious patron of goodness', whereas 'Jesus was crucified because he would have nothing to do with a political theology'. The primacy of the gospel had been betrayed, Dr Torrance alleged, and politics had been brought into Christian faith as well as into the Olympic Games. And the more 'involved' in that style, the less had church leaders been in touch with the common people and their spiritual needs. At a time when our society was being decomposed in its depths – Dr Torrance illustrated this from the disintegration of form in art – Christian thought was itself being trivialized.

'Christian theology must be concerned with the unity of structure and substance, form and being, and therefore with overcoming everything which divides them or tears them apart.' That scarcely seems a message for the man in the street. But Dr Torrance indicated three ways in which the theology he advocated was strengthening the church at levels deeper than any being touched by the World Council of Churches.

First, he drew attention to the dogmatics of Karl Barth, through whose influence 'we are learning to think together the being of God in his acts and the acts of God in his being'. The Barthian idea of being/acts is, Dr Torrance claimed, a richer and more powerful idea about the living God who reveals what he is by what he does; and in its power it is 'parallel' with the Einsteinian idea of space/time, although 'of course on a different level'. Second, he drew attention to the Roman Catholic liturgical movement, based on the idea of the church worshipping God through the 'vicarious humanity or human priesthood' of Jesus Christ. This widespread renewal of the church's self-understanding as the body of Christ at prayer is, he claimed, a richer and more powerful idea than any understanding of worship to be found among liberal Protestants. And third, he drew attention to the flourishing Pentecostal movement, which 'represents a recovery of belief in *God*, not some remote, inactive deity but the mighty living God who acts, and who interacts with the world he has made'. To this theological revival, both Catholic and Evangelical, the key was, he said, a deeper understanding of Jesus Christ as the one mediator between God and man, who 'mediates our access in the Spirit to the Father'.

In the later discussion, Dr Torrance recalled how as a young minister he had brought the gospel to a woman dying of cancer. Her doctor had told her that her flesh was 'full of corruption'. He was, however, able to assure her that the son of God had shared human flesh, and had really changed the human condition because humanity could now share his resurrection. She too believed, and after receiving the Lord's Supper died in peace.

The Unity of Believers

In the course of discussion, it became clear that Bishop Ramsey agreed with Professor Torrance's enthusiasm for contemporary science, and with his criticism of contemporary 'moralism and politicism which lacks depth'. His opposition was on two grounds. Dr Torrance seemed to be jumping too quickly from scientific to religious statements, without fully explaining his moves and without fully allowing that in religious statements 'the truths will not live up to the verities'. (Aquinas was quoted as saying after his mystical vision: 'All I have written is as straw.') And Dr Torrance did not give enough prominence to the changes which had been forced on religious belief by empirical knowledge. To sustain the second criticism, the Bishop referred to a prayer authorized in 1849 for use in a cholera epidemic, attributing the cholera to the wrath of God. He did not think that any intelligent Christian could now use that prayer.

Dr Torrance agreed with Dr Ramsey that theology should not be 'hard and prescriptive'. 'All kinds of changes have to be made in our traditional formulations of theology', he agreed. But he again urged that theology can and must be *descriptive*, describing 'what we really know of God and his relations with the world'. Whether such a claim for theology must always lead to conclusions different from Dr Ramsey's was left unclear. Challenged to relate his theology to the abortion controversy, Dr Torrance was not very explicit, except in emphasizing that God 'interacted' with the foetus and that 'no pragmatic end should govern our decision'.

Clearly those two theologians remained on good talking terms; and clearly the church in the twentieth century would have to accept and use both their approaches to its intellectual tasks. But the Church Leaders' Conference showed more than this. The unity of believers, experienced in its fellowship, was articulated more positively in the Bible studies which began each day in the large Cadbury Hall after the eucharists or prayers in the chapels of the surrounding colleges.

The unity was the more remarkable because the expositors of the Bible came from such different positions. The Dean of Liverpool, Edward Patey, seemed worried chiefly by his immense cathedral's grandeur amid such dire social needs: 'the church often seems to be a device for preventing us from taking either the world or God too seriously'. He spoke between Michael Taylor, the Principal of the Northern Baptist College who had recently been in trouble with some of his fellow-Baptists for an alleged Christological heresy, and John Stott, the Rector of All Souls, Langham Place, London, and the leader of the Conservative Evangelical movement in the Church of England. Other expositors included Professor Robert Davidson of Glasgow, who spoke about our spoiling of God's good creation ('it is easier to build cathedrals for worship than to live responsibly in the cathedrals of a God-given environment'), and a Jesuit, Robert Murray, who spoke from a humble heart about St Paul's vision of the new creation. 'There is only one thing we have to do, and that is not to break the tiny little link which we call faith; and if we have no faith we need it – but we can only ask for it.'

Of course there were great differences of tone. Having shared his worries with us, Dean Patey preached with the ringing assurance of faith in the essential: 'We have come together to learn not how to salvage an institution, but how to obey a Lord.' As he presented a psalmist's cry of exile or the crucified's cry of dereliction, Principal Taylor communicated his own integrity in responding to the world's question: 'Where is your God?' Sentence by sentence, John Stott worked through John 17 with the challenging assumption that it stated the wishes of Jesus himself for the ecumenical movement. But at no point was there any fundamental difference. Most of John Stott's exposition commanded the agreement of many who persisted in thinking that the chapter he expounded had not been composed by Jesus of Nazareth. And the whole conference was moved when the most lighthearted and optimistic teaching came from the speaker from the grimmest background: J. L. M. Haire, Principal of the Assembly's College, Belfast.

It became manifest that simply by reading the despairs and hopes of the Bible in the light of prayer and experience. Christians could attain a unity which crumbled when theology was done with a less close dependence on the scriptures.

4

The Spirit Disturbing the Churches

The Church as 'Us'

The willingness to go to a long conference where disturbing lectures had been arranged was itself significant. These church leaders had their ears close to the ground where the roots of church life grow slowly, but in spite of the natural tendency of all leaders to claim that the bodies which they lead are in good heart, these were openly worried men.

While in Birmingham many of the church leaders studied a British Council of Churches document published earlier that month. It was entitled *Stand Up and Be Counted*, and was mainly a plea for greater co-operation and accuracy in the collection of statistics. But it also gave church membership trends for 1961-71. The *Congregational Year Book* reported a drop from about 210,000 to about 160,000 full members, and the *Baptist Handbook* one from about 290,000 to about 240,000 (both for England and Wales). Comparable figures (in a population less than two-thirds the size) were given in Kenneth Slack's book as 457,000 Congregationalists in 1909 and 435,000 Baptists in 1906. Methodism, the Church of England and to a lesser extent the Church of Scotland are all known to be in decline numerically. Even the Roman Catholic population figures have levelled off. 'We are in a backwater', Miss Pauline Webb bluntly told the conference. But because these church leaders had stood up to be counted, they now sat down to be told.

No less remarkable was the agreement among these church leaders that in the disturbing wind of change the mighty Spirit of God was blowing. In the church as well as in the world, God seemed active as (in David Jenkins' phrase) 'the disturber'. Something like an ecumenical consensus of aims in a positive and strongly Christian response to the challenges of the Holy Spirit in our time emerged at Birmingham 1972.

Because the conference included such a wide variety of traditions, there were disagreements. How much of the existing organization of a church is God-given, and how much has been evolved pragmatically? How much is eternal, and how much disposable? The conference could not answer with one voice. Yet disagreements about such questions should not be allowed to obscure the fact of solid agreement about many aims. Because most of the people present carried pastoral and administrative responsibilities, there was also a constant recognition of the down-to-earth problems to be solved before the aims could be realized. Indeed, John Huxtable's sermon rang bells in many minds with its emphasis that a consensus at a conference was not enough. 'Do we intend to act upon such further light as we may have been granted? Or will it all end in talk? Obedience to the known is the path of illumination to the unknown.' And the very fact of this virtual consensus about aims should not be ignored in a fair assessment. When one remembers how many traditions and responsibilities were represented, one sees the consensus as little short of a miracle. 'Cut the talk and get on with the job' is an easy reaction for administrators and pastors to make; but this conference helped those of them who had ears to hear to understand more of what the job given by the Spirit today is.

The willingness to discuss these problems together, within the body of Christ, was also full of promise. Cardinal Heenan generously declared: 'All Christians who recite the creed must regard themselves as members of the Catholic Church.' But here he was being optimistic, and excessively so. In the *Church Times* on the eve of the conference, Canon David Paton of Gloucester offered a reminder of the individualism of many Christians. 'I am coming to believe', he wrote, 'that a lot of what we say about mission, about liturgical worship, about stewardship, and so on, simply passes many people by because it does not seem to be about Christianity as they understand it. To many people Christianity is a personal (which usually means private and individual) relation with God, and it is usually associated with a particular place. In this model of Christianity other Christians and the Church are there of course, but there is no necessary obligation to them ... They do not accept that the visible Body can require that obligation which is presupposed in virtually all the policies and programmes put to them.'

The reality of church life often bears out David Paton's sobering analysis. In a document circulated at the conference, Professor J. A. Whyte of St Andrew's recalled 'a congregation in a town I know, which was a dying cause, but it nearly killed two ministers. When the last one left for happier things, the congregation refused to unite with the church next door (literally, next door) and decided to disband. Even then, it insisted on disposing of its own property, rather than allow it to benefit the other church. I passed the building the other day, and on its Wayside Pulpit was the message, "Thou shalt love thy neighbour as thyself".'

During the conference a young social worker in Notting Hill, Chris Holmes, protested that '90% of the churches' resources goes into the buildings, yet they are empty for 90% of the time'. He pleaded with the churches to get out of their buildings into life. And in a deliberately shocking contribution, the Reverend Trevor Beeson told the conference that as a journalist (he had edited *New Christian*) he had read innumerable documents urging change and new life on the churches – with scarcely any result. So his one highly-loaded question was: 'Why have church leaders done so little to transform the church into an appropriate instrument for the kingdom of God? Are you too busy? Or are you afraid? Or is the church like a hospital ship which cannot be made into an aircraft carrier?'

But Trevor Beeson was not giving the whole picture. Sitting in this Church Leaders' Conference were Irishmen who had courted unpopularity and risked reprisals in order to blot out the record of their churches against reconciliation. At the time of the conference, leading British churchmen were receiving personal abuse because they had supported the British government's decision to fulfil the country's obligations to the Asians expelled from Uganda. Clergy and congregations were trying to produce homes and jobs for the refugees, and in London the officers of the Community and Race Relations Unit of the BCC were the elected leaders of the team co-ordinating the efforts of all the voluntary agencies. And these were not isolated cases of the vitality and involvement of the body of Christ in the 1970s.

The willingness to come together and to go out together – embodied in the sheer fact that this ecumenical conference was being held to face radical challenges – exists in many parts of the contemporary body of Christ. Professor Whyte wrote: 'We all know that congregations and kirk-sessions can often be shockingly short-sighted and worldly, more concerned about the damage the youth club might do to the premises than about the needs of youth; but these same people can just as often show an astonishing breadth and depth of compassion and care, giving time and money without stint in response to human need. I think of a young wives' group, which looked as if it might become a purely social affair, with hair-dressing demonstrations and the rest. It has now adopted a ward at a nearby mental hospital, and those young married women, with plenty to occupy them, find the time and energy to befriend these people in the most joyful way. This is grace and goodness – growing out of the soil of the church.'

In this paper Professor Whyte asked the conference not to add to the church's existing burden of guilt. He shrewdly wrote: 'I often hear ministers projecting their own sense of guilt and inadequacy on the congregation, so getting relief for themselves by increasing the guilt and inadequacy of those already in the pews ... A community of guilt cannot do a thing. It is paralysed, and all the exhortation in the world cannot set it free.'

Accordingly, under the leadership of a layman (Mr Mark Gibbs), the conference's commission on 'The Church as Institution' held a wide-ranging discussion; but it issued a report of only six paragraphs. Each paragraph concentrated on strengthening the grace and goodness already growing. Indeed, the concentration was even narrower than that. The commission evidently believed that the key to the strengthening of the Christian church was not far to seek. The key was in the already flourishing ecumenical movement. This widely representative group of church leaders took it for granted, and never bothered to state, that *together* Christians can grow and advance. The fact that this was taken for granted is one of the most significant and encouraging facts about Birmingham 1972.

'We ask', they said, 'for further development of ecumenical strategic planning, at all levels of our national life, in careful relationship with secular units of government and administration, and with proper techniques of fact finding and evaluation. At the same time we have been impressed by the painfulness of closing down churches and organizations (which was described to us as often "not death but murder"). *How can Christian people catch a vision of the wider church beyond their own congregation or committee?*

'The present development of so-called "areas of ecumenical experiment", ecumenical parishes, and similar ventures is raising many questions of membership. Strong views were expressed by some of our commission that it is now necessary for individuals and congregations to be enabled to belong to more than one denomination. *Is it not necessary to establish a national body to look into these developments?*

'We ask for a reassessment of the work of many church institutions in caring and service, and for great caution before the churches develop any new such institutions. We suggest that they should concentrate on (1) emergency aid, (2) pioneering work where the state or the community will not yet undertake this, and (3) finding ways of "caring for the carers", so that they can play a humanizing role in secular social care structures. *Do we care for people best ecumenically, or in denominational organizations?*

'We are strongly convinced that the churches must learn to invest less in buildings and much more in people – in education, training and support for both clergy and laity. Time and time again in our discussions we have been faced with the needs of the laity as they live and work in modern, secular society. Such education must include a more thorough, common search into the whole meaning of the ecumenical movement. *How can we overcome the great gap of understanding which still exists between the ecumenically committed and other Christian people?*

'The churches need to think out much more clearly the relationships between national, regional and local church structures, and between all these and informal groups of Christians. Communication between all these units of organization is often shockingly bad. *How can we quickly improve this?*

'We have been deeply concerned as to how to get "from here to there", how to implement the ideas we list above. There is so much tokenism and nominal support for such things as ecumenical projects and laity education that for many Christians church leaders and bureaucracies are fast losing credibility. We urge a sharp examination of what has been called each denomination's 'sovereignty' or 'empire-building' and the tendency very often to assume that we will only do together what we cannot (afford to?) do separately. *What a church is committed to is often revealed in its budget.*'

Or, as David Paton put it when this report was welcomed in a plenary session: 'Put your denominational money where your ecumenical mouth is.'

Half-way to 1980

Birmingham 1972 was reminded forcibly of the resolutions adopted by an overwhelming majority at the Faith and Order Conference in Nottingham in 1964. 'United in our urgent desire for One Church Renewed for Mission, this Conference invites the member-churches of the British Council of Churches, in appropriate groupings such as nations, to covenant together to work and pray for the inauguration of union by a date agreed amongst them. We dare to hope that this date should not be later than Easter Day, 1980. We believe that we should offer obedience to God in a commitment as decisive as this. Should any church find itself unable to enter into such a covenant, we hope that it will state the conditions under which it might find it possible to do so.'

The reminder sparked off two and a half sessions of free debate. At first some indignant speakers seemed to assume that nothing had been done to meet the 1964 challenge. The conference's own chairman, however, pointed out that the imminent union of the English Congregationalists and Presbyterians was 'more than nothing', and the Anglican Archbishop of Wales, Dr G. O. Williams, summed up the discussions based on the acceptance of the idea of covenanting for church union in the Principality. A report had been issued in 1970. Every possible care seemed to have been taken to make these discussions, leading to decisions by 1974, both deep and wide, both theological and local – and in both the languages of Wales. It was emphatically not enough, said the Archbishop, 'to sell the finished product to customers who don't see why it is needed'.

The Reverend Roderick Smith reported on the new conversations between the Presbyterians, Congregationalists and Anglicans in Scotland, while emphasizing the problems created by the vast numerical preponderance of the Church of Scotland (and by the historical associations of the word 'covenant' north of the border). In Ireland, too, the drafting of a definite 'Statement of Intent' had shown how amid the recent troubles the main Protestant churches had found themselves drawing closer and closer together, although emphatically not in any hostility to Rome.

Obviously, the main cause of frustration and despair was the breakdown of bilateral negotiations between churches. One example was the failure of plans to unite either the Episcopal (Anglican) Church or the Congregational Church with the Church of Scotland. Another was the abandonment of the official scheme for Anglican-Methodist reunion after the inadequate majority produced by the General Synod of the Church of England on 3 May 1972. This was what gave bitterness to the choirboy's remark quoted by David Jenkins: 'O come *on*, all ye faithful!' And this was what gave force to the same speaker's conviction that nevertheless 'God is getting on with the job' – in the rise of experimental churches and other new

Christian gatherings, and in all the progress of the gospel among groups which place themselves outside the church, so that 'church leaders go on making regulations about situations which don't exist'. David Jenkins pointed out that in the Bible 'prophecy is making sense out of a bad job after it has happened because you have found God in it'. So he urged the conference to theologize *after* the events creating unity.

The applause which greeted this call to action was a reminder of how many of these church leaders were involved locally in ecumenical co-operation, including the increasing use of the same building by worshippers drawn from different denominations (made possible by an Act of Parliament in 1969). Local ecumenism has grown immensely in Britain and Ireland since 1964. Its Anglican Archbishop remarked at this 1972 conference that the whole of Wales was fast becoming an 'area of ecumenical experiment'. Another bishop (unnamed) was quoted as happily expecting at the present time 'ecclesiastical anarchy'. In 1970 a report by opponents of the Anglican-Methodist union significantly combined conservative (Catholic or Evangelical) objections to the proposed Service of Reconciliation with a strong endorsement of bold local action, which seemed to its authors to be the best – indeed, the only – way of 'growing into union'. A session which was to have considered 'experiments in renewal for mission' had to be cancelled for lack of time, but R. M. C. Jeffery's book, *Case Studies in Unity*, is available as a picture and interpretation of the fast-changing local scene. And from all this local activity, several speakers now drew one conclusion: wherever possible diocesan and other denominational boundaries ought to be adjusted ecumenically. If they meant this seriously, the church leaders present had committed themselves to a major reorganization.

The pace of mutual acceptance between Christians at the Lord's table also seems more promising than the pace of official negotiations for a complete union. The invitation to all members of the conference to receive communion at the Sunday morning service presided over by the Archbishop of Canterbury accorded not only with the wish to be hospitable on an ecumenical occasion but also with a recent canon of the Church of England, officially admitting baptized and communicant members of other churches to Anglican altars. Nor was it all a one-way traffic. Prominent Anglicans who ten years ago would have held back communicated at the Church of Scotland service; and the Archbishop of Wales stressed what a quick and large change was involved in Welsh Anglicanism's current move towards reciprocal 'intercommunion' and the mutual recognition of ordained ministers. Nor were there lacking quiet Roman Catholic voices to hope that before long Rome would officially embark on intercommunion.

But is intercommunion between still distinct Christian congregations all that is really required? Some hold so, and they have had much influence. During the conference Archbishop Lord Fisher of Lambeth died. The conference mourned the passing of this churchman who contributed much to the ecumenical movement; and it heard a few echoes of his view that 'organic' unity such as the Anglican-Methodist scheme envisaged is, for the time being at any rate, the wrong goal. The well-known Methodist preacher, Dr Colin Morris, was quoted about the unimportance of reunion schemes in comparison with the urgent tasks awaiting Christians in the world; two sixpences meant the same as a shilling.

The Reverend Andrew MacRae, Secretary of the Baptist Union of Scotland, made an eloquent plea for caution in covenants or union schemes. He was not committed to any concept of reunion which would inevitably destroy the character of the present churches. He warned against haste – 'timetabling the Holy Spirit'. He also protested against any suggestion that deep differences of conviction should be ignored, and 'action' substituted. It was not realistic to expect Baptists to accept the baptism of infants, or the Sacrifice of the Mass. He pointed out that the British Council of Churches recognized the importance of its members' convictions by allocating its chief offices between the main denominations: there was, in fact, a 'power game' here. And he added for good measure that churches under bishops did not seem to expect the Holy Spirit to guide a united church to abandon episcopacy. No, unity must be sought by patiently drawing together Christians in Christ's way – and in God's good time.

Another warning came from Colonel Denis Hunter of the Salvation Army. His Army, he said, had retained the spirit of mission and therefore did not need to be troubled by questions of church union; and it was international, more sensitive perhaps to links between Salvationists around the world than to links with fellow-Christians in Britain, although a strong sense of Christian unity was continually nourished. He also reminded the conference of the Army's non-sacramentalist position – and quoted Bishop Hanson's Bible study that morning as indicating that the apostles themselves had probably not been baptized.

With equally good humour, Kenneth Barnes, of the Society of Friends, pointed out that the Quakers did not believe in ecclesiastical sacraments or in the primacy of doctrine, yet were constantly being told 'you are real Christians!' He recalled his own marriage to a Roman Catholic; and he thought that happy union was the best clue to ecumenical progress.

But the view that 'organic' union is the wrong goal was clearly a minority view at Birmingham 1972. Most of those who spoke to this Church Leaders' Conference displayed an interest in church union negotiations which was, in these often depressing circumstances, surprising.

The Archbishop of Wales emphatically rejected the theory that intercommunication was enough. 'If you believe that,' he said, 'come to some of our Welsh villages, where six churches or chapels stand side by side preaching the same gospel.' The youngest official delegate, Mark Williams, said that anyone who thought two sixpences meant the same thing as a shilling ought to try getting chocolate out of a slot machine. Alex Lyon, MP for York, remarked bitterly that reunion would be easier in time – because the churches if they delayed would get smaller and smaller. And several speakers thought that questions of the ordained ministry and the sacraments were no longer so divisive; so what were we waiting for? Kenneth Slack told the story of the ecumeniac who thanked God reunion would not happen in his time; and Dr Slack exclaimed, 'What is it that ripens time? *Obedience!*'

Voiced with brevity but passion, these were cries from hearts set on church union between the Anglicans, the Methodists and the Reformed, if not between others. It would be a union based on a common acceptance of God's grace – although no one advocated uniformity. At one stage it seemed possible that the feelings of the conference would sweep it into an endorsement of the daring hope of reunion for the member-churches of the BCC by 1980. But in the event, no resolution was proposed. The Reverend Peter Morgan (who edited a book of essays on *Unity: the Next Step?*, published just before the conference) pointed out that covenanting for union had never caught the imaginations of people in England. At the back of many minds in this Church Leaders' Conference was the possibility that the Roman Catholic Church would before long join the BCC. This possibility would grow less if a 'union by 1980' label were to be attached to BCC membership. Indeed, the differences and suspicions still existing between the Roman Catholics and the rest are such that on this sector of the ecumenical front a full union is not a realistic aim for the near future. It seemed more useful to use Birmingham 1972 for the expression of fresh hopes.

The first hope concerned Roman Catholic ecumenism, a growth-point of global significance. Immediately after Cardinal Heenan's lecture, which rightly or wrongly depressed almost the whole conference, Canon Bernard Pawley of St Paul's stated that the Roman Catholic Church numbered some 500 million, and constituted two-thirds of the Christian family. In all Christendom no church, he added, had done more to update itself. Cardinal Heenan himself pointed out the relaxation in the rules about 'mixed' marriages, and later on Bishop Alan Clark, Chairman of the Ecumenical Commission of the English and Welsh hierarchy, reminded the conference of the agreed statement recently issued by Anglican and Roman Catholic theologians on the eucharist, adding that a similar document on the ordained ministry was under preparation. But the conference experienced Roman Catholic ecumenism as more than a matter of rules and doctrines. A group of nuns, for example, led the worship one evening – and included a reading from Bunyan's *Pilgrim's Progress* in the service. One afternoon the conference heard a panel of five members from Ireland, Catholic and Protestant, jointly analysing their country's tragedies. A Roman Catholic bishop declared with heat that in Ireland 'the twenty-six counties need to be shaken up just as much as the six need to be reunited'. Above all, many conference members attended a Roman Catholic Mass in the George Cadbury Hall, and heard from some of their Roman Catholic fellow-members the hope that at the next conference of these dimensions the Roman Catholic Church would not only be a full member of the BCC but would also be able to invite all to receive the sacrament.

Members were therefore not surprised when, a few weeks later, Cardinal Willebrands travelled from Rome to Lambeth Palace and delivered a lecture full of charity and hope, looking forward to a time when Anglicanism (for example) would be in full fellowship with the Roman Catholic Church but not absorbed into the Roman Catholic system. On television the Archbishop of Canterbury hazarded the guess that such a reunion with Rome might come by the end of the century; but, he said, things were now moving so fast that it was dangerous to prophesy.

The second hope concerned Baptist participation in future conversations. Here, too, a full union does not usually seem a realistic target. But Dr David Russell, General Secretary of the Baptist Union of England and Wales, made a statement so important that it deserves to be quoted in full.

'It is not my intention to follow up the remarks of Mr MacRae except to say that, despite the difficulties he mentions, it is the deep desire of many Baptists in England especially to take part as fully as possible in multi-lateral conversations, that they may seek together the will of God for his church. But it is about another matter that I want to speak briefly now.

'It has been said in a report recently issued in the name of the the Roman Catholic Church in Scotland and the Scottish Episcopal Church that "the basis of renewal is to be found in a renewed understanding of the meaning of baptism" and that "the fact of baptism is the primary growth point in Christian unity". An illustration of this is to be seen in the recently agreed Baptismal Certificate approved by seven of our churches as indicating mutual recognition of baptism.

'It is a cause of great grief to many Baptists that this very point of unity is for us a point of disunity. There is so much in what is said by paedo-Baptists about the theology of baptism (even the wording of the Common Baptismal Certificate) with which we would readily agree. The difficulty for us is that theological understanding is interpreted with such different presuppositions and is applied to infants on the one hand and to believers on the other.

'There are some among us who feel convinced that we must interpret New Testament baptism as that of believers and practise it as such, and would ask for fresh consideration to be given by the other churches to the significance of that rite, so that we can find the way forward together. There are others, who, in the light of church history and the existing practice of the divided church, would in certain circumstances, such as the admission of members from other denominations, go further and be prepared to forgo this particular practice and accept the fact of infant baptism followed by confirmation as a basis of church membership. Even such Baptists, however, whilst recognizing their own weaknesses, would be troubled by the indiscriminate baptism of infants and would hesitate much on this score over committing themselves in the way I have indicated.

'I would simply ask that in future discussions on unity those church fellowships which differ from us Baptists try to understand our deeply-felt convictions in this matter and try too to sympathize with us in our dilemma as together with them we go on striving to know God's will for his church in this connection.'

The third hope concerned the Methodist attitude. The President and

Secretary of the Methodist Conference both made statements stressing that Methodism still seeks 'organic' union. A suggestion was made by an Anglican (Canon Horace Dammers) that the Methodist Conference should 'admit into full connection' Anglican priests who might in that way seek Methodist authorization, and it was announced that this suggestion was being studied. The President (the Reverend Harry Morton) welcomed bold discussion, while emphasizing that 'the recognition of ministries must be mutual' and that 'we are not willing to sacrifice the order we now have for a mess of pottage'. The Secretary (Dr Kenneth Greet) was emphatic that there had been, and would be, no recriminations on the Methodist side after the Anglican withdrawal, and that both churches should continue to respect each other's discipline. The Bishop of Chester firmly voiced the shame of many members of the Church of England at the General Synod's failure to endorse the union scheme – and the gratitude of all that Methodism had responded to the 'shared disappointment' so generously. (An Anglican listener could not help reflecting that it may have been within the divine providence to humiliate the Church of England by the fiasco of 3 May 1972. Perhaps Anglicans had to be made a laughing-stock before they could grow out of the idea that they held the key to reunion.) Roderick Smith prophesied that Methodism in Scotland would be united with the Church of Scotland (as a Methodist Synod) 'within three years'.

The fourth hope welling up from the experience of Birmingham 1972 concerned the United Reformed Church. Several speakers urged this church not to relax when it had set up house, not even to wait for all the curtains to go up. It should quickly issue invitations to multilateral talks about union with other English churches. Kenneth Greet spoke of Methodism's 'eager willingness' to accept a new invitation, and an Anglican of the younger generation, Colin Scott, expressed what appeared to be a widespread view that in England only the URC was in a moral position to take a fresh initiative.

John Huxtable, who was to become the United Reformed Church's first Moderator, now spoke from the chair about these sessions as the 'most encouraging' in the whole conference. And he spoke, too, of the hope that 'local ecumenism will work up a sufficient head of steam to make those who have national responsibilities get on faster'.

Do It Yourself

But what of the even deeper divisions, between conservatives and radicals (or modernists) arguing about the fundamental faith? Those who had hoped that this Church Leaders' Conference would issue a clear statement of a faith to be preached to the people were disappointed, and could only hope that some future gathering might get round to that, perhaps in the 1980s. The conference did not examine at any depth the substance of Christian faith. Both the lecturers and the commissions largely concentrated on questions about its style.

Had there been more willingness and time for doctrinal problems, even deeper divisions might have appeared. In an essay published a few days before the conference met (in the Cambridge symposium on *Christ, Faith and History*), Dr John Robinson contrasted a theology of 'two storeys' with one of 'two stories'. By this he meant that contrast between a theology in which the supernatural world (the Trinity, the angels, etc.) is regarded as being 'above' and as swooping down into the natural world (by revelations, miracles, sacraments, etc.), and a theology in which only one world is acknowledged – but this one world is described by telling symbolic or poetic stories about a mystery in addition to any matter-of-fact or secular 'stories' based on science. Had any such contribution been made to Birmingham 1972, the analytical cat would have been set among the theological pigeons.

Perhaps more discussions about doctrines would have led eventually to a substantial agreement. But the conference did not try very hard to reach theological answers (any more than Sir William Armstrong had tried very hard to find a congregation he could join without losing his intellectual integrity). Instead, being composed of pastors rather than scholars, it was preoccupied by the practical questions of how Christians are to live, and how the Christian church is to maintain its fellowship, amid the present uncertainties.

Looking back, one sees that this conference took some constructive and very important moves to bridge the gap between the two psychologies which seemed at times to be supporting two Christianities. First, it set the search for the real God within the attempt at real prayer. Second, it put the contemporary questions about Jesus alongside the traditional answers, and the answers alongside the questions, showing that questions and answers must now be held together in the life of the Christian community.

Listening to God and listening to one's doubtful or faithful neighbour: these were agreed to be the two most important ways of 'being open to the Spirit', a key phrase of the conference. These church leaders seemed to commit themselves to a greater emphasis both on informal prayer and on lay theology. They acknowledged an obligation to give more help to laymen who, like Sir William Armstrong, found the churches' spiritual and intellectual conventions far remote from the world they inhabited. But this help was not to be the mere repetition of the old teaching. Instead, it was to be an invitation to explore and to experiment in bafflement and faith: a do-it-yourself kit. To the outsiders' question, 'Where do we enter?' the conference's answer seemed to be: 'Wherever you want.' To the insiders' question: 'What of the bits I don't like?' the conference's answer seemed to be: 'Don't worry about them.' Mark Gibbard, leading an hour of quiet on the conference's last day, quoted Baron von Hügel's answer: 'You must be like the cows, who choose the grass they can digest.'

Of course the problems remained – and not only the problem of how literally to take the creeds. ('To say that Jesus rose from the dead is not the same as to say that John rose from his bed,' one speaker told the conference – and probably did not expect a rapid retort from a fellow-delegate: 'But it is *precisely* the same!') There is the problem raised by Christians who are aware of human emptiness and sin when prayer is commended as self-discovery. 'It is like unwrapping a parcel said Mrs Rosemary Haughton, the persuasive Roman Catholic writer on prayer. 'But I am not like an onion!' replied a Presbyterian minister who wanted something more. And there is the problem raised by believers in the transcendent God of salvation, when mysticism is commended as a communion with nature. An Indian bishop in the conference begged the West not to take Eastern mysticism so seriously; it was impersonal, it was inferior to the gospel.

But the conference was successful in providing some do-it-yourself kits, at least for its own members. Deeper than the disagreements was the shared experience of having met a real mystery in honest thought, talk and silence. A Methodist contributor to the panel on 'Spiritual Life Today', the Reverend Neville Ward, expressed the conviction that more mature forms of prayer were emerging amid all today's difficulties. Essentially, prayer for ourselves or others was a simple turning to God: 'thy will be done'. When the commission on 'The Real God and Real Prayer' reported to the conference, two Roman Catholic priests expressed the hope that a new depth was being given to the ecumenical movement in Britain by the concentration on faith and spirituality. Father Robert Murray spoke of the need to explore further the mystery of intercessory prayer, which to him was part of the mystery of Christian faith. Essentially, 'it is something Christ does not ask us to take part in'. And Father Patrick Murphy

O'Connor spoke of the need to form many ecumenical groups for the study and practice of prayer.

Professor John Macquarrie, who led this commission, stressed the task of 'co-theologizing' at every level in the life of the church, getting our minds clearer about what we believed and sharpening the church's understanding. But he emphasized also that the real God is the one to whom we pray. Ten years ago, he said, he could not have pictured himself speaking to a Church Leaders' Conference about prayer, for then the discussion of prayer had seemed 'unctuous and sentimental'. But he had come to see that prayer was at its heart 'letting things declare themselves to us in a new depth, so that we may become more truly the instruments of God'. The report which Professor Macquarrie drafted was the best document of the conference. (It is reproduced in this book as Appendix B.)

Reflecting on the work of the commission which he led on 'Who is Christ for Men Today?' Canon David Jenkins has written that 'some people were troubled that some statements should be questioned. Other people were troubled that some statements should be made at all or with so little questioning.' But because they were meeting as Christians, the commission 'assumed a common commitment in and through Jesus Christ to that which is ultimate'. They also assumed 'the existence of church and tradition as enabling, guiding and contributing to this commitment'. Their experience was therefore of togetherness in Christ as a common exploration with affirmations, questions and starting-points which differed for different persons and groups.

The diagram produced instead of a report by this commission began with traditional theological language: 'Jesus Christ is God incarnate, revealed as everliving Saviour, friend and Lord. Our authority for so believing is to be found in scripture, enlightened by the Holy Spirit in the fellowship of God's people.' But against this was the modern world's question: *How do you know?*

In what sense is Christ unique and of cosmic significance? Four subsidiary questions were seen to be involved here. 'How do we relate human identity and Christian identity? What is the relationship between the Spirit of Christ and men of other faiths? Are all men to become Christians or can salvation be pluriform? Is it conversation or conversion with men of other faiths?' And the commission made some concise affirmations. 'Jesus is not all there is to God. Christ is the man for others, leading to an experience of the transcendent; Christ is the light of every man. The need to love and to be loved is the basis of human identity. Experience of the transcendent is rooted in particular experience but must be shareable.' These affirmations were, as the reader will expect, followed by many questions.

But further affirmations followed, too. 'Jesus is a person with whom we have a relationship through our experience; through the New Testament witness; in the Christian community; and in the community as a whole.' The words 'released' and 'responsible' point to facts of 'experience' – although there is mystery in this relationship with Jesus and no one can speak adequately about it. What can be said is this: 'You cannot know fully, but you are known. Christ takes the initiative and comes with his own urgency. The church does not take Christ into the world; he is already at work there.' Someone in a plenary session suggested that the Jesus Kids' stickers ought to be changed to read: *Jesus is at work today*.

The commission's conclusion was that 'theology is the art of discovering models which will evoke the meaning of Christ'. These images must constantly be revised, yet models may yet again 'catch the light' so should not be completely discarded. Reassurance is possible; it means being sure that 'the Christian who moves onwards will find Christ' – in an activity which is 'always communal'.

Spread the News

The commission on 'Evangelism' was sub-titled 'Proclamation and Dialogue' because it was intended to bring together those who believe in the confident preaching of the everlasting gospel in order to produce conversions and those who hold that Christians ought to concentrate on serving their neighbours and (when there is a pause) on quiet conversation about what in the world God is up to. The commission's task was indicated in the names of those who assisted the Archbishop of Wales in its leadership: the Evangelical preacher John Stott, the radical theologian J. G. Davies, and (to stress the global dimension) Canon John V. Taylor, General Secretary of the Church Missionary Society. And in this task, the commission was successful.

In its own words, 'the commission was representative of all churches and schools of thought. The commission was agreed that, however the apostolic witness about Jesus Christ may be reformulated, Christian believers have an unchanging responsibility to share with all men in the discovery of the living reality of Jesus Christ and in responding to him. Through response to God in and through

Jesus Christ, persons individually and corporately are made whole ... Man's deepest need is to give himself wholly in love to God, in whom alone he can find fullness of life. Jesus has shown us that this implies loving our neighbour for God's sake. This is a costly calling, and involves all that is meant by social responsibility as well as personal spiritual concern ... There is only one mission of God in the world.'

'Proclamation and dialogue are not mutually exclusive,' the commission affirmed. 'By proclamation we understand the setting forth of the gospel as confirmed in personal experience, in spoken or visual form, in terms that others can understand. Proclamation will invite the "hearer" to respond to faith and repentance. Right proclamation is characterized by that openness to others and willingness to listen which are the marks of true dialogue ... Our medium should not deny or obscure our message, for example by pressuring people.

'There is a specialized use of the word dialogue which refers to converse about the things of ultimate concern between people of one faith and another, or of one faith and of no faith, and its object is the kind of understanding through which both parties hear the word of truth and mercy. Christ speaks to both partners; our hope depends upon his presence.

'Members of local churches need to be given confidence and understanding regarding both methods, but especially in regard to dialogue – which can be applied in informal situations where conversation, or "gossiping the gospel", is natural. Enabling Christians to participate in dialogue ... shall be a prime task of the churches' educationists.'

When announcing this agreement, the commission also drew attention to the document recently produced by the Joint Working Group of the British Council of Churches and the Roman Catholic Church on the once-vexed question of 'proselytism' or conversion from one church to another; and it called on the same group to initiate a further study, this time of Christian involvement in broadcasting and television, before the present charters of the BBC and the IBA lapse in 1976. The commission urged the churches to be more aware of the far-reaching effects of radio and TV and of the evangelistic importance of religious programmes. In particular, 'because local broadcasting depends largely on the local community, a great increase in the church's involvement will be necessary'.

This agreement about the one 'mission of God' was, some observed, predictable. But the commission's members had not done their previous work, or given their previous teachings, entirely in the spirit of the report they now presented; and the conference itself seemed at times unlikely to agree on any gospel worth either proclaiming or gossiping. The aims, once agreed, seemed obviously right – but first the aims had to be agreed.

It was only an agreement at a conference, others said. But the conference met at a time when the Spirit seemed to be driving the churches into mission together. The Birmingham Council of Christian Churches was at that very time embarking on a united local initiative to serve, and then talk with, the wider community. In other areas similar efforts were being made or planned. And on Easter Day 1972 a letter had been published over the signatures of the Archbishop of York, the (Roman Catholic) Archbishop of Liverpool and a leading Free Churchman, Dr John Marsh, issuing the 'Call to the North' – an imaginative programme of united evangelism. Christians all over the North of England were called:

'1. To use the coming twelve months to learn the meaning of the Christian faith, and how to relate it to mankind's needs.
2. To join in prayer for this purpose with fellow-Christians of all traditions.
3. To work out ways of making the Christian faith intelligible to those at present out of touch with Christian worship and activity.
4. To plan some definite acts of witness to the Christian faith, beginning where possible in Holy Week 1973.'

5

People and a Planet in Crisis

Involve Yourself

The involvement of the churches in political controversy has recently produced big headlines and hot arguments. On the one side are those who advocate a heavy involvement. Faced by the iniquities of apartheid and Portuguese colonialism, they urge that the churches have a clear moral duty not only to withdraw any money of their own invested in Southern Africa or in trade with that area, but also to discourage all such investments; and not only to defend and aid the victims of South Africa's racist laws, but also to encourage the guerrillas of the liberation movements by making them grants to be used for humanitarian purposes. The World Council of Churches has come down on that side. On the other side are those who are nervous – and in some cases can produce good reasons for their nervousness, for they ask what good these steps will do to the people of Southern Africa. And they see Northern Ireland as a hideous warning against any over-emotional identification of the Christian gospel and church with a partisan viewpoint in politics. Like Professor Torrance, they would prefer the World Council of Churches to concentrate on the spiritual depths and demands of the gospel. Between these two positions are many Christians who know why Christians should be involved in politics, but ask how.

The commission on 'The Churches and Public Issues' handled these hot potatoes. It was led by the Reverend George Balls, Convenor of the Church of Scotland's Church and Nation Committee until May 1972.

It was emphatic that in Britain and Ireland Christians ought to be involved in politics – partly because *all* citizens ought to be. Its report roundly declared: 'It is vital to the well-being of our nation and the maintenance of our freedoms that all should participate, to the fullest extent possible, in the processes of national and local decision-making which constitute the political life of this country. We believe that the people of these islands, if they wish to retain the freedoms which they presently enjoy, cannot afford the luxury of cynicism about politics but must be ready for an involvement which may – who can tell? – prove costly.'

So far from deploring controversy, this commission seemed prepared to arouse some more. It reported that 'there is often a tendency for individual Christians and for some of the churches and their official spokesmen to concentrate upon a range of personal issues which they regard as having a strong religious flavour, such as marriage, divorce, abortion, family planning, racism. But this is not enough. We call for a wider Christian concern. To give one example, we regret that until now little attention has been given by the churches to the Christian understanding of the economic and financial structures of our society. As a matter of urgent importance in the immediate situation of our country and as an element in the solution of many of the major social problems of the present age, we would urge the churches to put immediately in hand a Christian critique of the present economic and financial system. We see this as involving, amongst other things, a searching examination of the churches' own involvement in the existing economic and financial power structure.'

In the debate which followed, a welcome was given to this plea to update Christian social thought by bringing it into the Heath–Wilson, Walker–Armstrong era, and an approving reference was made to the recent studies of the economic system sponsored by the French Protestant Federation. But it would be false to pretend that Birmingham 1972 gave any clear indication of the lines on which a Christian study of basic economic issues should now be conducted. The conference was busy with many problems, but some of its silences were deafening. The menace of inflation was scarcely mentioned, and while the conference seemed highly suspicious of economic growth (for environmental reasons), no other alternative to the 'hard times' prophesied by Sir William Armstrong was clearly envisaged, apart from a new mood of self-denial which would constitute a major miracle in the British democracy. The word 'Europe' was a little whisper. It is to be hoped that the whole conference fully realized what a lot of hard thinking would have to be done before Christian social thought could return to the level reached at the Conference on Christian Politics, Economics and Citizenship held under William Temple's leadership at Birmingham in 1924.

So far from regretting the energies which the British and Irish churches have put into discussion of social and political problems at the national level, this commission called upon the churches to produce more resources for this work ('which its importance in Christian witness demands and deserves') – and called for new efforts to relate the churches to local government. 'We think that, in areas of the country co-terminous with local authorities, groups of Christians with particular knowledge and enthusiasm should be set up, not necessarily based upon local congregations but equipped to bring Christian insights to bear upon matters of social and political significance. This gap needs to be bridged as a matter of urgency, particularly as local government reorganization is likely to lead to a major restructuring – and alteration of content, or at least of balance and emphasis – in locally provided services.'

What might be involved in this plea for more contact with local government was brought home to the conference in a plenary session. One group reacted to the commission's report by offering a playlet in which a local Council of Churches was pilloried for failing to protest against the eviction of some gipsies. Up jumped a Labour councillor to make his own comment on this dramatized protest – which, he said, ignored the fact that a last-minute protest was usually too late. It was an effective comment, and it made the conference see the importance of the Caravan Sites Act.

In the debate, the Dean of Salisbury described this report as 'like the Venus de Milo – an overwhelming glimpse of the obvious'. But to whom would it be obvious? Perhaps even in Wiltshire the church's involvement in public affairs is not complete. So far from thinking that the churches were too obsessed with a 'social' gospel, this commission declared that 'the plain truth is that many loyal church people today have no more understanding or care for their duty as Christians in social and political witness than they have for their Christian duty to bring men to Christ. We see these tasks as two sides of a single coin ...'

'We recommend,' the commission reported, 'that men and women with the necessary enthusiasm and knowledge should be designated by the churches to inspire and activate. The theory and practice of Christian political involvement should be an integral part of the training of all theological students and of all programmes of in-service training. Similarly, a theological understanding of social economic and political issues should be part of all programmes of Christian adult education. The inspirers and educators (some full, some part-time) may be lay or ordained. Some few will work nationally, many more locally, and all, where possible, ecumenically. We look not for a new organization, but for the strategic placing of individuals.'

Miss Margaret Kane spoke modestly to the conference of her own work encouraging Christians in greater social responsibility in the North East of England. Many knowledgeable agitators like her seemed to be needed.

A Nation in Change

The commission on 'Social Change in Britain: The Christian's Response' (led by the Reverend Len Tyler, Principal of William Temple College), aroused appetites for the new tasks to which the churches were called. The lengthy notes on its discussions which it submitted to the conference cannot all be reproduced here; but the key points can be extracted.

'The fundamental basis of industry is changing', this commission reported. 'Once labour was industry's prime resource. Now industry relies increasingly heavily on capital and knowledge. The number of men and women who are unemployable – or who, though employable, are unemployed – is growing steadily. The previously successful Keynesian methods of restoring full employment seem no longer capable of meeting these problems. Are we moving into a society in which paid employment will be regarded, not as a right, but as an option open to sections of the community? Agriculture is one industry among many in which marked rises in productivity have been achieved with a radically reduced labour force.'

But increasing mobility and leisure have created immense psychological problems through 'the fragmentation of comradeship and common values' and 'the turning inward of the individual to his personal and immediate family concerns'. And although the economic gap between the affluent workers and middle class is disappearing, acute social problems have accompanied 'the emergence of a new under class composed of the bottom of the working class with large families, the unemployed, the disabled, the old.' Especially ominous is 'the identification of immigrant workers with the under class'.

This commission had found in the contemporary West a growing impatience with the meaninglessness of paid employment and frustration at the emptiness of enforced idleness – and it linked this with the widespread and sometimes violent rejection of the established order. The omnicompetent State is not the answer; access to the holders of power in the local community or work-group is more important. Spontaneous protest often seems more effective than conventional politics. The Executive appears now as 'the Beast' of Revelation 13 – a biblical chapter to be weighed alongside the deference of law and order in Romans 13.

But there are welcome signs in contemporary society of a new emphasis on the personal. Hannah Arendt has distinguished between labour, meaning all that is repetitive and cyclical (such as washing up); work, meaning man's control of his environment; and action, meaning personal relationships. The new emphasis on personal action was connected firmly by this commission with the Christian belief in the personality of God, which produces an understanding of human growth as 'the relating more widely and at a deeper level to other persons'. One comment at the conference was that the stress should now be not on the accumulation of material goods accompanied by inflation (and by environmental disaster) but on the cost of loving.

Faced by the 'massive problems caused by social change in inner city areas', this commission put to the conference the suggestion that the churches should raise a new fund to back up community development. The sum of £500,000 by the end of 1974 might be raised by 'appeals to individuals or congregations or by allocation from central church funds'. This suggestion was not acted upon in the conference, but delegates took it away as an indication of what might be involved if the churches meant business in responding to Britain's own social change.

Caring for People

The short report on 'Caring for People in Crisis' was presented by John Hare, Bishop of Bedford. It took for granted the dedication of church leaders to pastoral work – something which, incidentally, could not have been taken for granted in every previous period of church history.

Seeking a wider strategy of pastoral care, this commission spoke of 'the suffering and insecurity experienced when the even tenor of life is threatened or disrupted by social change or personal disaster'; but also of every crisis as potentially creative. Our time of crisis gives many opportunities for the fuller expression of the church's caring – and as many as possible must be involved. As Miss Christian Howard said in the debate, 'the churches are full of slightly inadequate people who can, nevertheless, help'. As the commission reported: 'Widows now seem to be the responsibility of the general practitioner. Yet sharing bereavement and its crisis can help a congregation, or any Christian, to grow ... A minister who appropriates all the counselling will impoverish his congregation, and the congregation could impoverish a local community by doing its caring for it. The needs of present society indicate the importance of Councils of Churches providing teams for pastoral care and counselling in places where previously individual denominations have taken separate initiatives. The establishment of ecumenical chaplaincy centres in universities and places of further education is an example.' And the carers must be cared for. At present there is all too little contact between preachers and social workers, yet this commission suggested that 'local Councils of Churches may be the best agencies to act supportively to help those engaged in all forms of local social work – both statutory and voluntary'.

In the discussion a Roman Catholic priest urged the simple and age-old duty of personal service; 'someone needs my time more than I do'. Probably he was preaching to the converted. Attention was drawn to the recent publication *50 Million Volunteers*, with its optimistic theme: 'Volunteering is fast ceasing to be an activity practised by a small minority for the benefit of the majority, and is becoming the natural means by which the majority of citizens may become involved in their own community.' One comment was that many of those volunteers for social work are lapsed Christians seeking to find a deeper meaning in life. They might be drawn by personal contacts into an understanding described by Bishop Hare (echoing Professor Torrance): 'We are more than do-gooders because we believe that the ultimate therapy is Christ.'

Michael Wilson, who is both a priest and a doctor, deepened the conference's debate by pleading for six shifts in our theological thinking. We needed to move from individualism to more corporate ideas – for example, a suicide was the result of a sick and sinful society; from the concentration on specialism and training to the truth in Nye Bevan's maxim that 'there is no substitute for the good neighbour'; from 'caring for casualities' to 'the creation of new life styles'; from 'crisis as disaster' to 'crisis as opportunity'; from the fear of death to faith in resurrection 'through the partial deaths of crises in daily life'. In these six shifts, a whole new approach to pastoral care was implied.

The Vulnerable Earth

The British and Irish churches are, more than any other large institutions in the national life, concerned for the poverty of the Third World – as the size of Christian Aid operations shows. The World Council of Churches is, as much as any other international body, consecrated to the service of the world's poor. At this Church Leaders' Conference, universal agreement on the Christian duty to help the developing nations could rightly be assumed. Apart from Bishop Luwum's lecture, the point was repeated not by words but by drama. The conference enjoyed the witty anti-racism of Sylvia Read and William Fry in *Lovely Day for the Race!*, was made to think by the BBC film *South Africa Loves Jesus*, and was moved by the Christian Aid film, *Out of the Darkness*.

In the agenda of the commissions, preference was given to a subject much less familiar to the churches. The commission on 'Man's Stewardship of God's World' was led by Hugh Montefiore, Bishop of Kingston, and the experts who addressed it included Barbara Ward, whose recent book, *Only One Earth*, was regarded as essential reading. As a result of careful discussion, this commission eagerly shared its convictions, but avoided hysteria.

'We accept', they said, 'that the resources of this planet are limited, that its life-support systems are vulnerable, and that the combined effects of modern technology, wasteful consumption and population growth can place all life on earth at risk. We accept that the preservation and protection of both man and nature require the redirection of technology, the re-ordering of consumption and the limitation of population growth on a planetary basis. We are convinced by the weight of evidence, particularly that produced at the UN Conference on the Human Environment at Stockholm, that these changes are necessary.'

'We are also convinced,' the commission added, 'that there is an urgent need to bridge the gap between the rich and the poor. The hope that world economic growth will produce sufficient wealth for all is proving illusory. In any case, economic growth as currently measured is now inadequate as a yardstick of well-being. The re-ordering of human consumption must involve a massive re-distribution of resources, both within our own society and on a world basis, so that the fundamental needs of the present and the future human family for health, food, shelter, employment and recreation can be met.'

In response to this planetary crisis, the commission provided a clear summary of Christian insights. 'The world is created by God for his pleasure and for man's enjoyment. Nature must be respected as such.

God himself has sanctified the world through his Incarnation in Jesus Christ. Man, created to be the child of God, has evolved within nature and belongs to nature. All men are created in God's image. They are accountable to God for their use of his world, and are co-workers with God in it. Man, through his thoughtlessness, greed and presumption, reflected in his misuse of science and resources, has done violence to the harmonies and balances of nature. By his substitution of size for value he had distorted, as with a cancer, the natural and healthy proportions of nature. The situation demands repentance, expressed in a radical reorientation of human attitudes towards nature, man and God. God through Jesus Christ gives Christians the hope that, by divine grace, man can enjoy a healthy relationship with his environment. Our greater hope is that God's purposes for his world will not be frustrated by man's disobedience and folly.'

The commission called for urgent studies of national policies to be worked out in response to this crisis and in the light of these insights, recognizing that the policies needed to avert catastrophe will 'require fundamental changes in our present economic order'. It asked the British Council of Churches to encourage more Christian thinking in consultation with experts, suggesting among the topics to be covered: the development of technologies appropriate to genuine national needs, including the needs of developing countries; the recycling of resources: the discouragement of the built-in obsolescence of products, and the artificial stimulants to unnecessary consumption through advertising; the pricing of products in relation to their total (including environmental) costs; the expansion of public transport and an equitable limitation to private transport; the imposition of upper limits to personal income and consumption; a national population policy; the reduction of expenditure on weapon systems; the development of international agencies, and the spread of environmental education in schools and elsewhere. As starting points, the important declaration of 'non-governmental organizations' at the 1972 UN Conference on the Human Environment, and the current 'Society, Religion and Technology' project of the Church of Scotland, were both commended to the churches' attention. Mention could also have been made of the current World Council of Churches studies and of the Church of England report on *Man in his Living Environment* – or of Bishop Montefiore's own trenchant paperback, *Can Man Survive?*

The commission, not content with words, urged on Christians to participate in group action to promote environmentally sound development, and to protest against legalized environmental outrage.

Be Simple and Share

Two attempts were made at this Church Leaders' Conference to sum up its thinking in words which might be simple and powerful enough to reach far.

The first attempt originated in the commission on man's stewardship of God's world. It asked the church leaders to show by their own examples that 'environmental responsibility and social justice on a global scale demand changes in personal, as well as national, ways of life'. The commission therefore urged church leaders 'to pledge themselves to a simplicity of life which is generous to others and content with enough rather than excess'; and it put before them some points which could help others towards simplicity of life.

'Question your own life-style, not your neighbour's!' But on this healthy basis, some definite suggestions for 'waste-watching' were made. 'Where you have a choice, resist obsolescence and choose the longer lasting; resist wasteful packaging; support public transport; question advertisements. If possible, work out your way of life with the help of others (family, friends, congregation ...), asking such questions as: "How can we measure our real needs – by the standards of our neighbours or by the needs of the poor? How can we be joyful without being greedy or flamboyant? How can we be good stewards without being overscrupulous? How can others benefit from what we have? How far does our personal way of life depend on society's wealth? Can our society's way of life be simpler? Is there any one such change we ourselves can work for?"'

So this group asked all its fellow-Christians to make decisions about personal budgets (or the size of the family) as citizens of the planet. It offered these points to ponder: 'Happiness is knowing what I can do without'; 'My greed is another's need'; 'Am I detached from worldly goods if I keep what I have, and want to add to it?'

The second attempt to sum up the relevance of the conference was made on the last morning, when the young, radical commentary *Upside* was distributed to delegates. This final issue suggested seven slogans or mottoes to the church in the light of the conference. I reproduce and italicize them here, although I have been so bold as to change the order in which *Upside* printed them. I have also added (not in italics) the commentary which I thought was needed to explain them when I read them out in a pulpit on the next Sunday.

'1. *Not to expect to know more until we have been obedient to what we do know.* Many people at this Church Leaders' Conference expressed great impatience with the talk, talk, talk in the British churches. There was a powerful feeling that we in the churches know pretty well what we ought to do. What we lack is the will to do it. Until we put into practice more of the insights which we have, we shall not receive, and we shall not deserve, fresh insights.

2. *Not to confuse agreement with unity, or certainty with faith.* The conference, because it was representative, found itself divided theologically. But there was also a unity of spirit after some painful experiences, and we learned that Christians can live in unity even when they disagree about many things. However, we also learned that in the present state of theology and the church Christians have to put up with a great deal of uncertainty. The things about which we all argue are few, although they are vital; and even these things are not exactly certain like mathematics, but are matters of faith, of trust, of vision.

3. *Not to deal with people in crises, but to share crises with people.* The church must never be aloof or patronizing – for it is in a major crisis itself. We must all identify ourselves with a world full of problems, with other people in crisis. Christians must take off their protective clothing and wash feet.

4. *To make decisions with others and not to make them on their behalf.* The old style of authoritarian leadership is out, and this conference showed it. We must develop a new style of real consultation springing out of real fellowship. Only so can any decision-making rest on people's consent. Only so will the brave talk in the church lead to brave action. And only so will the church be a helpful example to the nation.

5. *To do nothing apart which can be done with the community.* This means that we should not be in a hurry to demand that a Christian label should be stuck on good work; instead, we should rejoice to see that the job is being done. For example, the Welfare State now does much work which used to be charitable work done in the name of the church; but that is good. What Christians can contribute is their humble service wherever good work is being done – that, and also their own pioneering wherever a new service is needed.

6. *To shift attention from the church's struggle to survive to man's struggle to be human.* So often we are tempted to concentrate on the

protection of buildings and congregations almost as if we were maintaining a network of private clubs. But what matters is the doing of God's will, and God's will is that men and women everywhere should rise to the full height of their humanity. The prosperity of the church as an institution matters a great deal less than the coming of God's kingdom on earth. The gospel we proclaim is about the kingdom; it is not chiefly about the church.

7. *To live more simply so that others may simply live*. This is the last motto or slogan, and it is the most challenging of all. It calls upon Christians to avoid all extravagance because so many millions of people in the world today do not have enough. We ought to support movements such as Christian Aid and Oxfam even when it means self-sacrifice. As a nation we must be more clearly a champion, not an exploiter, of the poor. And this generation has to discipline itself in its treatment of the resources of the earth, so that food and fuel and delight may be handed on to those yet unborn. As members of the Christian church and as members of the human family, we must so live now that there will be a future.'

In such words, many fresh challenges to action came out of this conference. What was missing was a simple gospel which could be shared; a clear spiritual message which would arouse, persuade and convert because it had first aroused, persuaded and converted the church leaders themselves. On the other hand, Birmingham 1972 was to many who took part in it an authentic experience of the Holy Spirit. It taught openness and humility, and it gave energy for the ecclesiastical and secular tasks of the future. It gave energy, too, for the religious quest and its necessary sequel, a vital theology – more difficult even than new negotiations for church union or a new prophecy about the economic system. At least these church leaders seemed ready to turn afresh to the Bible, to the Spirit and to the planet, and so to the future. Theologically they were in the mood of Hamlet – 'if it be not now, it will come: the readiness is all'.

Some words spoken to the conference on 12 September came alive with a double challenge when the man of God who spoke them, Ian Ramsey, Bishop of Durham, died on 6 October: 'A crisis of faith there is; but if we respond aright we can play our part constructively in the emergence of a new culture and a new era, and meanwhile we can show that the gospel points to an authority, a security, and a purposiveness which is fulfilling and not tyrannical – that for which our society is searching ... Today I see the possibility of advancing with all the vision of the pioneer, the pilgrim, the man of faith, who endeavours to talk of as best he can, and in his practice to display as best he can, that which inspires him, that which called forth and constantly renews his commitment, and points him forward to fulfilment. It is a critical time, but for that very reason it is a time in which we should be glad to be alive. "This is the day which the Lord hath made; let us rejoice and be glad in it."'

APPENDIX A

A Roman Catholic View

by B. C. Butler, OSB, Auxiliary Bishop of Westminster

It seems almost impertinent to add anything to Dr Greet's splendid retrospect of the Church Leaders' Conference. My excuse must be that what follows comes from a Roman Catholic, and this conference was the first of such great occasions in this country in which the Roman Catholic Church took part with full membership.

In the deepest sense, it was a pastoral conference; an enquiry and a reflection in the hope of discovering how the churches can best serve the cause of Christ in these islands and in the world today. It is a cause for great thankfulness that it did not confine its attention to the care of committed Christians, but had in view the wider needs of the world. The theme was not primarily the church's unity, but the church's mission to mankind.

It is, however, impossible to collect together 500 leading churchmen of nearly all the Christian bodies in this country without being faced with the problem and the scandal of our divisions, and it was quite proper that ecumenical questions came to be asked in public before the end of the conference.

As usual, both theological and non-theological factors were found to be implied in our divisions. I was in the commission whose theme was 'The Real God and Real Prayer', and the differences of spiritual approaches there disclosed were by no means all the expression of different theologies! I think that one of the most potent dissolvents of non-theological obstacles to unity is just that getting-together in mutual respect, friendship and living discussion of which the conference was such a remarkable example.

The days at Selly Oak did not, however, weaken my conviction that theology is extremely powerful, both for good and evil, a conviction that came to me during the second Vatican Council. I think that it is particularly powerful for evil in circumstances in which the interruption of full visible communion tempts people to maintain their own theological traditions and insights at the cost of inveighing against and rejecting those of others. I am sure that our present dedication to seek unity should carry as a corollary a determination to try to understand, appreciate, and so far as possible assimilate the insights of those from whom we are still separated materially, though no longer in heart and will.

In this connection, I want to suggest a thought that has come to me. It is very commonly supposed that the recovery of theological consensus is a prerequisite of the recovery of communion. I think it is often further supposed or implied that our divisions are effects of theological divergence. There may be some, though not full, historical truth in this. But I am inclined to think that, at the present day and for most of us, our theological divergence is the effect of our loss of full communion. I think that many a good Lutheran would be a good Calvinist if he had been born and brought up in a Reformed church; and vice versa. I suspect that many Roman Catholics would be ardent Anglicans – and vice versa – but for the accident of their birth.

For this, among other possible reasons, I suggest that theology needs to direct its special attention today to the theology of communion. I would distinguish the model of the church as 'communion' from the model, too exclusively used by some of us in the less recent past, of the church as 'society'. 'Society' suggests governmental institutions, delegation of powers, law, and a certain rigidity of structure. You will not suppose that a Roman Catholic sees no values in all this! But 'communion' is a much more flexible notion, more adaptable to aspirations for the widest possible diversity in unity. It is also, I think, a more basically religious concept. The bond of love seems both deeper and more fully Christian than the bond of law. I should myself say that there is subordination between the two concepts: society is for the sake of communion, not communion for the sake of society. I further think, as I have already hinted, that theology (or as I prefer to say doctrine) is an outcome of communion, rather than vice versa; this, at least when we are considering doctrines less fundamental than the reality of God and the uniqueness of Christ.

Logically, such thoughts lead on to a tentative suggestion. In actual practice, the conditions for full communion get laid down by Canon Law or its equivalents. But Canon Law is inevitably coloured by the circumstances in which it gets formulated. I think that we are living, in this ecumenical century, in a set of unprecedented circumstances.

Nearly all the great Christian bodies, which have almost gloried in their differences and their tendency to diverge still further from each other, are now on converging courses. Should we not be prepared to revise our 'Canon Law' conditions for communion, thus acknowledging in practice the truth that doctrinal consensus is as much the effect as it is the cause of external unity? These ideas may be familiar to many who have worked the ecumenical field in depth. They are perhaps somewhat challenging as coming from a Roman Catholic. I only put them forward here with hesitation, and for consideration.

Meanwhile, we all experienced in the Birmingham conference the reality of a communion which, though not yet (unhappily) full, was yet most real and most enriching. There was a unity of faith deeper than our differing formulations and theologies. There was charity, the very bond of unity. And there was a more than natural hope; a hope which perhaps we were too slow to recognize and to make our own – though Dr Greet in the end felt able to say that the ecumenical goal was not only possible but inevitable. We thank all those who conceived and organized the conference. And we thank God.

APPENDIX B

The Real God and Real Prayer

by John Macquarrie, Lady Margaret Professor of Divinity in the University of Oxford

The real God and real prayer – these are intimately connected and the commission was determined from the beginning not to allow their discussions to be separated into a theological or philosophical consideration of God on the one hand and reflections on prayer on the other. The real God must be a God to whom prayer can be addressed – this is part of the meaning of 'God' and God-language would not be appropriate otherwise; but prayer is in turn guided and kept authentic by knowledge of the real God.

The title given to the commission apparently carries some implications. One would scarcely speak of the real God and real prayer unless one supposed that there are also false gods and inauthentic forms of prayer. The title also implies that there is indeed a real God and that real prayer is possible. Similarly the title of the conference itself implies the reality of God.

We are committed as church leaders to the reality of God and prayer. The question was put to members of the commission whether they could conceive of a form of Christianity from which God and prayer had been eliminated. The overwhelming majority could not. We then asked ourselves why this belief is important – what is its cash-value, so to speak. We agreed that if God is only an abstract idea, then the belief does not seem to be important. But if God is a living reality with whom man can be in communion, then this makes a vast difference to our way of perceiving the world, to our 'feel' for the world, and to our patterns of behaviour.

In some respects this response was surprising and we have to pause to ask what it means. Only a tiny minority of the commission openly declared that God had become for them a meaningless word and prayer had gone completely dead, though they mentioned meditation on the words and acts of Jesus. Does this mean that the 'death of God' type of theology has slipped into the past? Or does it mean that among our church leaders (mostly rather senior) this position is not represented? In any case, it did seem a pity that there was no possibility for dialogue with those people in our churches who claim that belief in God and likewise belief in prayer in its traditional forms have become stumbling-blocks to some who would like to come into the Christian fellowship. Our feeling was, however, that people who could not as yet believe in God might possibly grow into fuller belief, for no one of us can have a full apprehension of the faith. Some things are clearer to us than others. But because something is unclear to some members of the Christian community, it should not on that account be eliminated.

For we were all willing to acknowledge our questions about God and prayer, even if we also affirmed that both God and prayer are essential to Christian belief and practice. The state of the church, we believe, is better described as bewilderment than scepticism. The sources of this bewilderment are complex, and certainly one cannot blame a few supposedly *avant-garde* theologians for upsetting people's beliefs. A neuro-chemist in the commission related the state of mind of Christians to a much wider bewilderment in the world today. Things are happening so fast and landmarks disappearing so swiftly that people are suffering from unprecedented emotional stress and a great deal of anxiety is being engendered. One of the casualties of this emotional sickness is religious faith.

We agreed, therefore, that even if the title of our commission seemed to imply that we might assume the reality of God and of prayer, we must begin from the beginning, and in particular we must try to stand alongside those for whom faith and prayer had gone dead. And first we had to ask, 'What do we mean by "God"?' What, for instance, do we mean when we affirm that Christ is God?

As first approximations, we got such answers as 'God is the ultimate point of reference' and 'God is the one with whom we have to do'. When, therefore, we say that Christ is God, we are at the simplest level asserting his ultimacy and saying that above all he is the one with whom we have to do. It was noted that even secular theologians who profess to disbelieve in God sometimes assert the ultimacy of Jesus Christ, and that this is at least part of what it means to call him God. If we try to see Jesus in abstraction from the Father, we get a mutilated concept of him, and certainly one that is at variance with the New Testament. It was noted also that of the two expressions quoted, 'ultimate point of reference' and 'the one with whom we have to do', the first is more obviously intellectual, the second more personal, and that both aspects have to be kept together in our thinking about God.

This is clearly only a modest beginning. Where do we go next in seeking a fuller understanding of God? There were several answers.

1. *Experience.* Perhaps most members of the commission claimed to ground their belief and understanding of God in experience. The many 'varieties of religious experience' seemed to be represented among us. Some spoke of the sense of the mystery of life; others had experiences of a more frankly emotional kind; others could speak of a sense of the presence of God – and it was noted that a sense of God's absence is also important, for one could not experience anything or anybody as absent unless somehow already related to that entity. Important, too, and in line with some recent theological thinking, was the stress on a divine dimension in all experience as well as in those specific moments of so-called 'religious' experience. But we clearly had to face the question of how such experiences can be tested. We were reminded more than once of groups such as the German churchmen who supported Hitler and sincerely believed that this was consistent with their Christian profession. The history of religion has been filled with delusions, though equally there have been people who have had a genuine experience of God without recognizing it. What tests are there? It was claimed that one test is growth towards Jesus Christ, specifically growth in the Christian virtues of faith, hope and love. More broadly, we might say that it is growth towards fuller personhood or truer humanity, of which Christ is the criterion. This is an empirical test of sorts. Furthermore, the experiences of the individual must be brought to the community for comparison and testing alongside the corporate experience. The recognition of the need for testing and criticism is, of course, nothing new, and other tests too are required if we are to guard against individualism and subjectivism. This brings us to the next point.

2. *God's acts in history*. It was strongly maintained by some of us that God is known first and foremost in his mighty acts recorded in the Bible, with the paschal mystery of Jesus Christ as the centre. This, it was claimed, is something objective. It is not subject to the vagaries of individual experiences. It was conceded, however, that the biblical witness to these acts of God is not always clear or, it would seem, consistent. And some had difficulty about the whole notion of an act

of God in history. How does one recognize it? Again, can we accept at face value the interpretation which the people of Israel put on such events as the deliverance from Egypt? Is there not as much ambiguity and uncertainty in history as in individual experience?

3. *Nature*. Although in the past nature has been considered an important source for the understanding of God, very little was said about this on the commission and it would seem that the appeal to nature is not in favour at this time. In general, it was agreed that any way of understanding God and his actions must be consistent with the understanding of nature given in the sciences. But there was in turn doubt about what this understanding is. It would be hard or impossible to believe in a God who acts in a world mechanistically determined throughout. But ours is a universe which has brought forth persons and they have reason and freedom so it is not a closed universe. (More was said on this topic by the commission on 'Man's Stewardship of God's World'.)

How are these different approaches to an understanding of God related? At first there might seem to be a sharp opposition between the appeal to experience and the appeal to scripture. But these are not finally opposed. We could hardly understand scripture's talk of God unless there were moments in our own experience where God-talk is appropriate. On the other hand, if we are to know the real God, then we must let our individual experience be judged and corrected by the God who came among us in Jesus Christ. The different paths to God converge.

The God to whom scripture testifies, God the Father of our Lord, has priority over every individual experience of God. Yet it may be that in trying to communicate what we mean by 'God' to someone for whom this word is not yet meaningful, or in trying to help someone who has lost faith in God, our first move will be to appeal to that person's experience – perhaps just his ordinary everyday experiences, helping him to discover in these a divine dimension.

Beyond this, we felt the need to construct a concept of God. To be sure, this need was felt more by some than by others, but we remained true to our decision not to separate theology and prayer, so that those whose interest was chiefly in theology were not allowed to avoid discussion of prayer, while those who wanted to get on with prayer were made to face the intellectual problem of God.

We recognized the limits of our enterprise. Clearly, the commission cannot be expected to come up with a concept of God that will solve the problems that have vexed man for centuries. In any case, we recognize the mystery of God – not a blank mystery, but a reality only partially glimpsed and always breaking out beyond our concepts. Of course, a reticence about God is nothing new. Theologians have always recognized that God transcends all our thinking of him, and there has been the long tradition of negative theology.

It was at this point that we were forced to recognize the pluralism of the contemporary world, including the church. Whether this pluralism is provisional or has come to stay, we do not venture to say. There are several concepts of God in current theology, all, we believe, consistent, some more, some less, with the Bible, yet using different categories and different models. Such, for instance, we find in process theology (Ogden, Pittenger, etc.), in some forms of existentialist and ontological thought (Tillich), in evolutionary theology (Teilhard de Chardin) and in the scientific theology of Torrance. While these are in conflict at various points and while it is not being suggested that one is as good (or as bad) as another, it should be recognized that all of them may have caught and directed attention to some aspects of the mystery of God. Furthermore, there does seem to be a 'family resemblance' among them that differentiates them from some of the traditional forms of theism. These new forms of theism stress the living God, his dynamic being; furthermore, they stress the intimate connection of God and his creation, not in any pantheistic way but in ways consistent with God's entering into his creation in the incarnation. Such dynamic conceptions of God are also very much in accord with the Trinitarian idea of God. The triune God is no dead or inert God, but a God whose very being is a dynamic diversity-in-unity.

We must stress that pluralism (or pluriformity) in theology must not be taken as a warrant for indifferentism. There is no prescriptive theology valid for all times, but theological discussion must go on constantly so that we may move towards a deeper understanding of God and our relation to him.

On the other hand there was a revulsion in the commission against what might be called the 'deistic' conception of God – an idea which has undoubtedly crept into our churches but which is less than Christian. It separates God from the world in a dualistic way, so that there is no true interaction between them.

The question was asked whether God, as conceived under these models, is a God to whom prayer can be addressed. It must be stressed again that the attempt to conceive God as more intimately related to the world is not pantheism, nor does it reduce him to some impersonal life-force or anything of the sort. It is so far from making prayer harder that it brings us to a truer understanding. Our prayers are not attempts as it were to influence the will of a distant God, but rather to let God pray in us, to let him work in the world through the praying community. It will be understood, too, that a God to whom prayer can be made is not less than personal. The interesting point came up that whereas some of our youngsters are turning to Indian mysticism because the prayer life of our churches seems to be so barren, many Indians have welcomed the Christian understanding of God as personal, for this brings a whole new understanding of prayer. Personal analogies, like all others, are inadequate to the reality of God, but they are the least inadequate.

The subject of pluralism soon came up again in our discussions of prayer. It was noted that much worship and prayer of the most authentic kind now goes on in small groups rather than in the large assemblies. We shall consider some reasons for this in a moment. It does seem to some of us, but not all, to indicate that 'in each place' it is likely that there will always be several worshipping communities, no doubt coming together for unified acts of worship and witness, but also maintaining a diversity. The meaning of Christian diversity is one that badly needs to be studied more thoroughly, not least in any discussions about Christian unity.

No doubt this diversity arises partly through temperament and training. Some of our group find most satisfying the traditional structure of prayer in the eucharist and the daily office; others prefer a 'secret discipline', as Bonhoeffer called it; others objected strongly to the use of the word discipline and even to set times of prayer, saying that prayer arises spontaneously in their dealings with others and in concrete situations. Theologically, this diversity surely arises from the richness of God himself who is seeking to meet man in many ways and many situations. Pastorally, this diversity opens up several avenues towards those whom we may be trying to help to pray. Just as at the present juncture we thought that perhaps God can best be spoken of to people first in terms of their own experience, so possibly the introduction to prayer might take place not through set forms or a fixed discipline but at least to begin with, in concrete encounters. But since we all have to learn prayer and openness (for these things need time and practice) it may be that we shall come to some kind of discipline, understood as a freely accepted pattern of learning.

We have, however, attempted to get beyond the sheer diversity of modes of prayer to some underlying unities. Let us begin with a few contrasts:

– Prayer through the human encounter and prayer as turning to God
– Prayer to God found in any place, prayer to God in the church or sanctuary
– Prayer and action
– Prayer as a continuous state of mind, prayer at given times
– Religion as a depth-dimension of all experience, and the specific religious experience.

While one or other side of these contrasts might carry more importance for particular people we do not see them finally in opposition, any more, let us say, than the belief that God is everywhere conflicts with the belief that there was a specific incarnation. The contrast between prayer and action, let us say, has been compared to 'shifting the weight'. There is no genuine prayer without action, yet all truly Christian action is guided by prayer. The specific act, the special time, etc., can be considered as foci or times of concentration.

We do not offer to the conference any packaged answers to the difficult problems we have considered, nor do we propose any high-sounding resolutions. But we think we have been helped to clarify our minds through our discussions together, and we hope that this will in turn help us to clarify the minds of others.

We would ask the churches to consider with great seriousness and sympathy the many movements in the past few years in several continents which have brought countless men and women to a revival of religious experience and Christian life. We think of Pentecostalism in its several aspects, the Jesus people, the renewed interest in retreats, groups for prayer, study and action, the rebirth of contemplation, worship festivals and the discovery that Christianity means celebration, with dance movement and drama as well as prayer, proclamation and song. These may seem sometimes to be irregular, but we cannot doubt that in some way they are 'of the Spirit' and that through them he speaks to the churches. They evidence the manifold richness and variety of the life of the Spirit and the desire born of deep inner necessity to find a way that is one's own and yet both related to the gospel of Christ and travelled in such movements. It is important, too, that the swing away from secular Christianity to the new spirituality should not lose the sense of involvement in the world.

The comparative 'success' of these movements, so far from allowing us to ignore the theological task demands it, if only because some of them validate anew the great Christian doctrines and – if they are to be saved from error and excess – demand that all our spirituality be measured by the full proportion of faith.

We have already referred to the dynamism of the Trinitarian conception of God. This is given practical expression in real prayer and worship, which is *to* the Father, *through* the Son and *in* the Holy Spirit, and thus is neither a Jesus cult, nor an 'enthusiasm' divorced from the 'scandal of particularity' and the adoration of the transcendent, any more than it is a bloodless deism. Some for whom traditional forms have come alive again feel that this is also expressed in the time-honoured relationship of eucharist and office. The eucharist is supremely the 'Jesus prayer', the solemn recalling of Christ, the worship of the Father through the Son; the office, austere and bereft of elaboration or ceremonial, is our acknowledgment of the hidden and mysterious God of whom 'our safest eloquence is our silence' and yet who has revealed himself in Christ. Both are real prayer only through the action of the Holy Spirit, who takes the things of Christ and reveals them to us, and comes to the aid of our weakness, so that we, who cannot find adequate words to express either our faith or our true needs, are bold to cry: '*Abba*, Father!'

The longing to recover community also presupposes a Trinitarian conception of God which delivers a man from ultimate loneliness and yet retains personal identity. But in our eagerness, and our realization that love of God and man are so inextricably conjoined in the gospel, we must not neglect the transcendence of God, so that, as well as our desire to make worship a genuine encounter between people and a real fellowship, there must be affirmation of the divine 'otherness', 'the beyond in our midst', yet always 'the beyond'.

We are perhaps in a better position than the generations of the immediate past to perceive that in a sense the only real prayer is the prayer of Christ in the church, 'the communion of saints', and that our private prayers, which may vary in their times, seasons and methods, are but extensions of that. But we would hope that our deliberations could help to a new understanding both of penitence and intercession in the life of prayer. Confession is not an attempt to induce unhealthy feelings of guilt, nor to nag the congregation into social concern. It is an acknowledgment of our humanity, of our share in the terrible frustration of the race, and a turning to God through Christ, so that he may look on us as found in him and we may share in his offering to the Father. Intercession may include something of the protest and complaint of scripture against the injustices of the world. But Christianly and positively it has as its basis our faith in the love of God declared in the forgiveness of sins which embraces all men, everywhere, and draws them into the communion of saints.

We repeat our conviction that the real God and real prayer are at the heart of the church's life. If these are allowed to be neglected, then we must expect the church to become increasingly ineffective and increasingly bewildered at a time when she ought to be leading men out of bewilderment. The churches today have many concerns and engage in many good works, but the priority belongs to God. If the church would move the world, it needs a place to stand – and only God transcends the world. It is the real God whom we have learned through Christ who alone should be allowed to write the agenda for his people, and we ought to be learning that agenda through real prayer.

BIBLIOGRAPHY

The mains books mentioned in the text are:

David L. Edwards, *Religion and Change*, Hodder & Stoughton 1969
R. M. C. Jeffery, *Case Studies in Unity*, SCM Press 1972
Alastair Kee, *The Way of Transcendence*, Penguin Books 1971
Hugh Montefiore, *Can Man Survive?*, Fontana Books 1970
Ernest Payne, *Thirty Years of the British Council of Churches*, BCC 1972
Arthur Michael Ramsey and Leon-Joseph Suenens, *The Future of the Christian Church*, SCM Press 1971
Kenneth Slack, *The British Churches Today*, SCM Press 1970
Barbara Ward and René Dubos, *Only One Earth*, Penguin Books 1972

Christ, Faith and History, Cambridge Studies in Christology, ed. by S. W. Sykes and J. P. Clayton, CUP 1972
The Eucharist: an Agreed Statement, SPCK 1972
50 Million Volunteers, HMSO 1972
The Fourth R, National Society/SPCK 1970 (The Durham Report)
Man in his Living Environment, Church Information Office 1970
Unity: the Next Step?, ed. by Peter Morgan, SPCK 1972

INDEX

of speakers and commissions